The Trials of Jesus

The Trials of Jesus

MEDITATIONS AND SERMONS FOR LENT AND EASTER

Frederick W. Kemper

Publishing House
St. Louis

Concordia Publishing House, St. Louis, Missouri
Copyright © 1977 Concordia Publishing House
MANUFACTURED IN THE UNITED STATES OF AMERICA

Library of Congress Cataloging in Publication Data

Kemper, Frederick W
    The trials of Jesus.

    1. Jesus   Christ—Passion—Sermons.   2. Lutheran   Church—Sermons.
3. Sermons, American. I. Title.
BT431.K45   232.'6   76-40444
ISBN 0-570-03743-3

To Agatha
my gift from God

Foreword

/ THIRST

The trial and damnation of Jesus is filled with more agony than anyone will ever know. He was squeezed out of His church on a false charge; outlawed by His nation without an indictment; *TEMP* sent to the ~~gallows~~ *Cross* by humanity without a conviction; and abandoned by His Father who chose to love us instead of His Son. In a symbolic sense, the clause from the Creed "He descended into hell" could well describe what happened on the other side of "dead." No word ever uttered by a human being is fraught with such terror or such despair as Christ's, "Eli, Eli, lama sabachtani?" *THE CROSS* *I THIRST* *THESE WORDS FROM*

This is the raw material that compelled the writing of the midweek series of "meditations" that comprise the first part of this volume. The meditations and the Easter sermon may be presented by one narrator, or by two in dialog form; in the latter case use the designations *A* and *B* to indicate changes in the speaking parts.

The series of sermons on the "Cross" are Sunday morning sermons (but quite usable on Tuesday or Wednesday, too). They demonstrate a way of thinking. Once you have determined that there is a straight, taut, thin line from the Father's Word at Christ's baptism to the "Eli, Eli," where His "baptism" ends, and that Christ walked this narrow line without wavering, His whole ministry takes on an almost overbearing coloration. He may have been the life of the party at Cana, but He did the first sign that pointed to His cross there! He may have been transfigured on a mountaintop, but He was not allowed to step over the line into heaven. He may have received the Palm Sunday approbation, but He knew "it was for His mighty deeds" (says St. Luke). He may have had His private angel messenger in Gethsemane, but the answer to the prayer He prayed there, brought by messenger, was "No!" He may have celebrated the Passover with His disciples, but that very night

7

the caterer placed the Passover Lamb on the table directly in front of Him. The darkness on Calvary may have sheltered Him from the merciless sun, but it was a symbol for the merciless judgment of the Father. Death, when it came, was kind.

No wonder Easter is such an exciting celebration. The war is over and done with. Satan is bested; death is conquered; sin is covered; freedom is assured. Because He lives, we too live and will live. Blow fanfares on the trumpets and let the descant to all of heaven's hymns begin. "Worthy is the Lamb to receive power and riches and wisdom . . . !" Let His holy church echo loud and unendingly: "Alleluia! Alleluia!"

The unifying word for the second series of sermons is "cross." It is used with a double entendre in each case. There may be "cross winds" blowing between two people; they "blow" Christ to the cross. There may be "cross words"; the redeeming Christ is eventually drawn into them. On Easter the cross is the cross, for it has become the highway to the Victor's crown.

If from my balcony seat in glory I see people whose lives I touched in time seated somewhere near the throne and am privileged to watch others arrive from time to time, I will be most happy. That's all this preacher wants—to speak the Word well enough to his people that the Holy Spirit can use it to create and sustain their faith and trust in Jesus Christ, his Lord.

Frederick W. Kemper

Meditations for Lent

I

"Who's on Trial Here?"

John 18:12-13 (KJV)

A Dear and beloved ones,

We are about to encounter the passion story of our Lord Jesus Christ once again. This is our annual encounter with the greatest event in the history of mankind. These are deep and serious days, for the history we are about to review is history filled with the power to condemn and the power to save.

Any encounter demands at least two participants. In this encounter *God* comes sweeping at us in the story of the Passion. In this encounter *Christ,* the crucified One, Christ, the redeeming One, comes to stand before us. It is important how we handle ourselves in this confrontation, for our life, our death, and our eternity depend on it.

In these devotions the encounter will be in the form of a "trial." The trial of Jesus will be part of it, but it will be broader than that. We will be examining the people of the trial—

"Who's the Victim?—Who's on trial here?"
"Call the witness to the stand"
"We find Him guilty"

—people like that. Right now, in this devotion, we want to take a good long look at the Victim. The question is—
"Who's on trial here?"

B The battle in the Garden of Gethsemane is finished. Jesus has wrestled with God in the deepest recesses of His soul. He has lost the battle, but He will win the war. The instructing angel comes to minister to Him, but also to point Jesus to the cross. There is no alternative to The Plan.

He stands in the Garden waiting for the temple guard. He

11

announces to the guards that their search for Him is ended. Judas, to fulfill his part of the bargain, plants a kiss of death on Jesus' cheek.

The Victim is unquestionably identified. There is no mistake, no false arrest. This is the Man marked for death!

They bind His wrists. Leather thongs, no doubt. Tight. Hampering circulation.

The bonds will be on Him for some time now. They will be there when the high priest's soldier strikes Him. They will be there when Pilate's soldier strikes Him. They will be there until they bring the oaken beams of His cross to be carried to the hill. There they will be replaced with nails. And the nails will hold Him until He dies.

A There is the preliminary examination in the house of the high priest. He stands bound before this judge. On the grounds that "It is expedient for one man to die for the people" He is brought before the Sanhedrin.

He stands bound before this tribunal. The witnesses, intimidated or paid, perjured themselves. The accusation is blasphemy. The penalty is death.

He stands before the king. The king satisfies himself that this Man is no threat to him. He has his little joke, and thus passes sentence. King Herod sends Him back to Pilate, a splendid robe draped across His shoulders.

He stands bound before Pontius Pilate. Pilate weasels out of the responsibility. In a tragic gesture he washes his hands of the matter. Jesus is condemned without charge.

He hangs bound to the cross. He is standing before the final Judge. For the first time in the trial there is an indictment. The charge is SIN; it is the rebellion against God; it is broken relationships. The charge demands the death penalty. The charge demands—banishment in hell. The sentence is irrevocable. It is carried out in darkness; it happens in deadly silence out there on the skull-shaped hill.

B The nails bind Him to the hour of His death.

A Jesus, the sinless One, is on trial in the passion account—but

12

He is Victim. Yet, is He really on trial—when there is no charge, or when the charges are patently false?

⚶ Remember His life—how He looked on a young man and loved him . . . how He saw the crowd and had compassion on them . . . how He had sought the allegiance of the Pharisees . . . how He had reached out for Judas . . . how He had taught men to know the Father aright.

ʙ Victim? Yes! On trial? No!

Who then is on trial?

And the answer to that question comes welling out of the passion story, and out of its purpose, and out of its accomplishment.

Everyone is on trial, the record says. Every one of His judges is—Annas, Caiaphas, Herod, and Pilate. Every one of them weighed the life of the holy Victim against his own needs. And in every instance Jesus weighed light. Every one of them is bound with the thongs of sin.

"Keep the church together; let no carpenter's son disrupt its unity," the high priests reason—at best. "He is touching us in the pocket-book," the high priests reason at their worst. Balanced against Jesus the traditional image of the church, or the bank account, tipped the scales. As they robbed Jesus of His dignity, His integrity, they stood condemned. They are bound with greed!

ᴀ "Who's this, John the Baptizer?" Herod wondered. "Do me a miracle!" he demanded. When the proof he demanded wasn't produced, when his fears had quieted, he looked at his scales. "What's one life?" he asked as, smiling, he sent Jesus back to Pilate. Poor Herod, his scale was faulty, but he preferred it that way. He stood condemned. He is bound by his need for pleasure!

ʙ Now Pilate. In the name of justice (heaven forbid!) he balanced Jesus against Barabbas. In the name of peace at any price he ordered a scourging. In the name of self-preservation he washed his hands of the matter, or, to keep the picture, he blindfolded himself against the death of the innocent One. He stands condemned. He is bound by his need for place and position.

13

A   And the Victim carried His cross out to the hill.

B   Well, now, that was an easy way out of a sticky situation. The church wasn't concerned enough, a king wasn't strong enough, justice wasn't really equal after all. The whole business was grossly unfair, but it's done at last.

A   Or is it?

B   There is other Scripture to contend with before we dismiss the trial. We still haven't found the culprit—but we will the moment we read a little beyond the passion account in the Word. "He, who knew no sin, was made to be sin for us," it says. He blotted out "the handwriting of ordinances that was against us, which was contrary to us, and took it out of the way, nailing it to His cross."

A   Who's on trial here?
    You are! I am!
    You might not understand it, but you had better believe it. Adam's sin bound your wrists. Your own sins bound your hands. Sin holds every one of us in bondage. We are the slaves of sin; we are under the dominion of sin. We are bound, whether we believe it or not, just as tightly as Jesus was bound.

B   But look! They untie Him. They place a beam on His shoulder. They nail Him to a cross. He cries from hell.
✳   He stood in our place—under the judgment of God. He stood there, for us. As they loosed Him, and as the cross embraced Him, He was embracing the whole world—and you—and me.

A   We were on trial that day. In Him we are acquitted. Our hands are loosed, like His, to embrace the world, to serve the world He served.

> Grant that we Thy Passion view
> With repentant grieving
> Nor Thee crucify anew
> By unholy living.
> How could we refuse to shun
> Ev'ry sinful pleasure

Since for us God's only Son
Suffered without measure?
Amen.

B The peace of God, which passes all understanding, keep our hearts and minds in faith in Christ Jesus—and endlessly rejoicing that He has loosed the bonds of sin from us—and ceaselessly reaching for the world with our freed hands. Amen.

II

"Attorney for the Defense"

John 7:40-52 (NEB)

A Dear and beloved ones,

Someone has said that a man in solitary confinement, or a man on the torture rack, needs only a ray of sunshine through a chink in the wall to keep his sanity. Surely there is some truth in that, for sunshine is our endless reminder that there is a world outside with its freedoms and with its people who carry the milk of human kindness to the brother in distress.

In the account of the last days of our Savior's life the Holy Spirit did not record a single ray of sunshine to which Christ could fasten His hope. From beginning to end it is a walk downward, as every recorded event depresses the suffering One in its turn.

B Could we try for a moment to find a ray or two?

A There was that angel in the Garden of Gethsemane! There's a bit of sunshine for you! But wait. Read between the lines a little. Jesus had been in long and earnest prayer communion with the Father. He had called the Father by name. The whole event was fraught with deep struggle, but it was communion. And when it was over the Father said, in effect, "Messenger boy (angel), you go down and strengthen Him." There is not much sunshine in that.

Or there was Pilate's wife. "Have nothing to do with that just Man," she pleaded with Pilate. Sunshine? Rather Procula was worried about her husband and what involvement with Jesus would do to him. "That just Man" was not the issue.

Or Simon of Cyrene, the man who carried the cross out to the hill. What a generous thing to do! But even in the case of Simon, the Spirit closed the chink when He carefully recorded the facts.

16

"Him they compelled to bear the cross," and against his will Simon took the beam out to the hill.

B There is no sunshine! There is no hope! Every step, every moment is a step, a moment down toward hell.

There was no relief. No wonder someone said He died of a broken heart.

A It is precisely this pathway, walked in obedience and in His so great love, that freed us from the burden of our sins, from the fear of dying, and from the terror of judgment. He walked that pathway to hell and death in our stead, and in doing so gave the "ray of sunshine" that has sustained the endless train of martyrs in their martyrdom, the long procession of dying Christians, the myriads of those who have mourned at the deathbeds of the saints. It is because of what He has done that the missionary in some far-off land has been sustained, or some Christian, caught in the continuing temptation to compromise, has kept his faith. It is as the Light appears to fail at Calvary, that it burns brightest; it is as God dies on the hill, that the glory of God is most glorious!

B Every man has the right to defense. Even the Sanhedrin recognized that. A trial before the Sanhedrin demanded by law that, unless there were witnesses in favor of the accused, no sentence could be passed!

Search the record! There is no man who comes to the defense of Jesus. There is no man to plead His cause. The voices for the prosecution are insistent and persistent. There is no voice for the defense.

A There is no voice unless you go back to the day the Sanhedrin met after an attempt to arrest Jesus had failed. John recalls it for us in our text. The church leaders gathered together to hear the report of the temple guard. So impressed had the soldiers been by the message and the authority it had been delivered in, that they had neglected to carry out their assignment.

B There is an uneasiness in the gathering.

A The soldiers have been "taken in" by Jesus.

B The discussion moves back and forth between the august members of the body. The gist of the discussion forms up. None of the *leaders* have been "taken in" by Jesus. Not one that they can think of. The *rabble?* Yes, they have been swayed. But then, the crowd couldn't care less about the Torah, they didn't know the Law and the Prophets. You couldn't expect more from them. But the leaders—not one of them.

A But there *was one!* He sat over to the side and cringed at the conversation; he trembled at the direction toward which events were moving. He had been "taken in" on the night when he had sought out Jesus to ask some questions. It was still night for him, but he could see the first glimmer of sunshine to his morning.

His mind was churning, and his heart pounding. He must say something. He must come to the defense of the Christ! But what? To say too much would ruin the perfect score to the Sanhedrin. To say too little would not help Jesus.

B He asked for the floor. He was given permission to speak.

A We have found our attorney for the defense! There is someone to speak for Jesus. He is right there in the Sanhedrin, too.

B Plead His case, Nicodemus. Plead long and hard and clear! Jesus has opened windows for you! He's given you a whole new perspective. He's Israel's one big hope, and Israel needs hope.

A The attorney speaks.

B From somewhere to the right or left, he opens his defense. He puts the defense in the form of a question.

"Does our law permit us to pass judgment on a man without a hearing, without facts?" he asks.

A That's an excellent question, Nicodemus! It is extremely tactful, but it does open up the issue. These men have to face themselves and what they are doing with a question like that!

B Press the point, Nicodemus. Make them answer and save Jesus from death. Give them the facts, Nicodemus. Tell them how He confronted you as the Messiah.

A "They" answered his question with a question. There was sarcasm in it; there was a sneer in it; for Nicodemus it was devastating.

B "Are you a Galilean?" they sneered.

A Its barb put the would-be defender on the defense.

B He backed down. He dropped the case. He chose sides. (Pause) It was the wrong side.

A Our Jesus, on whom we have staked our lives, in whom is our hope on our judgment day, through whom the dividend of heaven is given to us—our Jesus still needs defending.

B Outside the church, men use His name for cursing and men curse Him.

Inside the church, He is being stripped of His glory, His deity, His saviorhood. They allow a Jesus to have walked our earth, to have died on Calvary; they do not allow God's Son to walk and die for the sins of people.

A The call, the need, our Savior had in the days of Nicodemus are not so much changed. He needs still the man, the woman, the child, to defend Him in His daily trial in the world in which we live.

B And that means He needs you and me. Against the odds (which are against us), the sneers (which hurt us), we are still His defense in the 20th century.

A What kind of a defense are we making for Jesus? Isn't that the question the text is asking?

B Yes, what kind of a defense are we making for our Jesus?

A   Then, for all that wrought our pardon,
           For Thy sorrows deep and sore,
           For Thine anguish in the Garden,
           We will thank Thee evermore,
           Thank Thee for Thy groaning, sighing,

19

For Thy bleeding and Thy dying,
For that last triumphant cry,
And shall praise Thee, Lord, on high.
Amen.

B The peace of God, which passes all understanding, keep our hearts and minds in faith in Christ Jesus. May He fill us with the Holy Spirit, and in Him give us courage to defend Him. Amen.

III

"Call the Witnesses"

Romans 8:32 (KJV)

A Dear and beloved ones,
  To what lengths will a man go to achieve his ends?
  To what length will love drive a person?
  What choice does a man make when it is between another and his own son?

B Questions like these need answers. Each one of us ought to sit down and figure out what his answers would be—and are.
  God the Father was faced with these questions. He had to ask Himself (as it were), How far does My love go? The choice is between My creatures and My Son. Which shall I choose?
  Our text gives the answer.

A God spared not His own Son, but delivered Him up for us all.
  The choice was between mankind and Jesus. Many—most all—would have said, "Mankind be damned" and had an end to it. Not so our Lord.
  We who have been redeemed by the shed blood of that Son do not make that kind of choice for God. Judas didn't! Peter didn't! We don't.
  But God did! And that's the point of our whole faith. God made that kind of a choice for us.

B We can watch the whole awesome business work out in the passion story.
  God is absolutely relentless in it.
  He is the "Prosecuting Attorney" in it. Well, He is in a sense, at least.
  Let's watch!

A The disciples sleep a stone's throw away from the praying Christ.

Jesus is in agony. His knuckles are white with the tension of His prayers. The perspiration runs from His brow. Again and again He argued His case.

"Father, do I have to drink the cup of suffering? If You want, I will. Must I drink it?"

Over and over again.

"Father!

"Father!

"Father!

"Let this cup pass from Me; but Thy will be done."

B There is action at the last—negative, distressing action. An angel comes to minister to Him.

The Father, God, has begun the prosecution. He has cut Himself off from the Son. Now it is an angel. Soon it will be dread silence and darkness.

A God spared not His own Son, but delivered Him up for us.

B The sound of flesh on flesh in a room at the high priest's home as one of the officers strikes Jesus.

"Answerest Thou the high priest so?" the soldier demanded.

A No angel was there to intercept the blow. Are You sure, Father, that the angels have charge over Me, to keep Me?

B God spared not His own Son, but delivered Him up.

A Lies. Lies upon lies. Witness upon witness. Lies upon lies, in a steady stream.

At the last there came two who said, in effect: "This Man has blasphemed God." This Man must die.

B There is no voice from heaven. If there was, no one heard it, least of all Jesus. There is no "This is My beloved Son, hear ye Him!"

Silence in heaven.

The Prosecution has won a point.

A God spared not His own Son, but delivered Him.

B You do not throw Your pearls before the swine. You don't do a miracle when King Herod demands it. You stand there and let him come to a decision. You can count on the decision. It came.

Herod sent Jesus back to Pilate.

He became a kind of political football. He is an issue too hot to handle.

Pass Him back before you get burned!

A The Prosecution is pressing its point. Jesus is nearer the death penalty than He's ever been.

B Flog Him. Crown Him with thorns. Spit on Him. Slap Him. Humiliate Him. Make Him scapegoat.

Then, seeing that nothing works, wash your hands of Him.

Don't condemn Him. No pronouncement: Guilty! Just wash your hands and let Him be crucified.

A It's time for the twelve legions of angels, Father. Send one. Send Gabriel or Michael. It's not too late to stop what is happening.

Mr. Prosecutor! God! How can You? Father!

B God spared not His own Son, but delivered Him up.

A It's out on the hill, now. Perhaps the soldiers kick aside human bones to keep from stumbling.

The crowd looks up and mocks Him.

The physical pain is excruciating.

"Do a miracle."

Breathing is almost impossible.

"If Thou be King, save Thyself!"

B Then darkness, and stillness, and fear.

A There is silence in heaven.

The Prosecution has closed the door. The case is closed.

Jesus is in hell.

B The darkness stretches into an hour. Into two.

Into three.

A A cry rends the stillness.

"My God, My God, why hast Thou forsaken Me?"

And darkness closes in again, and stillness.

B God, you see, spared not His own Son, but delivered Him up for us all.

A The Prosecution rests.

B Jesus was made to be sin for us. In His unfathomable love He stayed steady on the course that justice demanded.

A The justice of the Father must be satisfied. His justice forced the cry from the very depths of Jesus' soul. Justice was done.

B *For us.* In our stead. Suffering what we should have suffered. Dying our death. Living in our hell.

A That's how far God's love went—for us. That's what all the bother was about to get us back into the Kingdom, under His rule, giving Him our allegiance.

B That's what God did to achieve His ends. He wanted us to live under Him in His Kingdom, freely, because we wanted to. He went all the way.

And when it came to a choice between Jesus and you—and me—He chose us!

A The Prosecution won its case. Thank God.

> By Thy deep expiring groan,
> By the sad sepulchral stone,
> By the vault whose dark abode
> Held in vain the rising God,
> Oh, from earth to heav'n restored,
> Mighty, reascended Lord,
> Listen, listen to the cry,
> Hear our solemn litany!
>
> Amen.

B The peace of God, which passes all understanding, keep our hearts and minds in faith in Christ Jesus. May He fill us with the Holy Spirit, and in Him give us courage to defend Him. Amen.

IV

"Call John Doe"

John 18:15-27 (KJV)

A Dear and beloved ones,
"I don't know, Lord—I just don't know!"

B Peter, that enthusiastic disciple, stands outside, warming himself. Inside, the high priest draws himself up to his full height to begin the questioning process. His aim is to move Jesus through the courts and out to the hill. He is judge, and in this pretrial session in his home, the judging begins.

The night air grows chillier, and Peter moves a little closer to the fire. Inside Caiaphas moves into his problem. He attacks Jesus from an angle: "What about Your disciples, Jesus of Nazareth?"

That was a good question. It would indicate the strength of the movement. It's a common question, too. We ask the same one often, and with just as impure motives. "How fast is the Unitarian Church growing?" (Is it a threat to us yet?) "How does the Lutheran Church stack up?" (Are we growing faster, giving more? Is the preacher really working?)

Perhaps this was involved, too. "How intense is the loyalty of the disciples?" Are they fanatical in their devotion? Would they follow through to the death? If so (reasoned the high priest), we have to approach the problem before us with the idea of a whole line of martyrdoms, and that would make some real problems.

Apparently Jesus didn't answer the question. If He did, the answer is not recorded.

A Peter stands silhouetted in the uncertain light of flickering flames.

B Caiaphas tries another attack. "Tell me about Your doctrine, Jesus of Nazareth. What are You teaching? How well are You

25

staying in the traditions of the fathers? How are You interpreting the prophets?"

Jesus speaks. It is the first time He speaks in His own defense. He makes His apology before Annas. "I spoke openly to the world, in the synagogue, in the temple. In secret I have said nothing."

This is the picture: "Wherever I have gone, I have spoken for all to hear. I have never conducted a secret meeting; nothing has been done behind locked doors; I have never plotted and schemed in a dusty room with a wobbly table and a dirty water glass. Everything I have said I have said in the open. The temple doors, where I have spoken often, are open twenty-four hours a day. In the temple I talked new concepts, new ideas. In the temple I sought to reinterpret the fathers for you, for it is in the temple that these things are done. The same has been true in the synagogues. The doors are not locked in the synagogues. In the synagogues I followed the practice of synagogue worship. In secret I have said nothing."

A Peter, his chiseled face caught in the light of a firebrand, is recognized by a servant girl. "Art not thou also one of this Man's disciples?" she asked.

B Jesus continues His defense before the high priest and the world.

He does a frightening thing. He lays His life, His death, His very Kingdom on the line. He stakes His defense on the man in the street! "Ask them which heard Me."

Imagine that! "Go out and get anybody who has heard Me speak and put him on the witness stand. I stake My life, My Kingdom on what he will say." Imagine that! Every hewer of wood, every drawer of water, every tax collector, every seller and buyer in the marketplace—if they have heard Me speak— will come to My defense.

A Peter, man of faith, man of action, answers the servant girl. "I am not one of His disciples!"

B Translate Jesus' call for witnesses into this year of our Lord. Every bus driver, every housewife, every student, every factory or government worker—every Sunday school child, every

26

church member, bring them in and put them on the witness stand. I stake My Kingdom, My life, on what they'll say.

Imagine that! Jesus reached right out of the trial, right at the beginning of it, and tapped you on the shoulder. "Come, John Doe, take the witness stand in My defense."

A At the fire a wind catches the coals and the flames leap up and light the faces of those gathered around the brazier. Peter's face is caught in the light again. Someone recognizes him. "Art not thou also one of His disciples?" he asks, not unkindly.

B "Come in, Peter, and take the stand in defense of Christ." Jesus' life is on the line. The kingdom of heaven is at stake. Come in, John, Susan, Bill, Mary, whoever you are, and take the witness chair for Jesus. Tell about His doctrine; tell what you know and believe about Him.

A Out in the courtyard Peter gives his answer to the question asked by an innocent bystander.

B And what about you? You have been in Sunday school for many years; you have sat year after year in your accustomed place in church; you have a Bible in your home. Give answer! Stammering, you speak. "Me? I'm not a theologian. I'm not trained. I never talk religion or politics. Me? On the stand for Jesus?" We move a little closer to our comfortable fire. "Me? An evangelist for Christ?" We lean over and blow on the coals. "Not me, Jesus!"

And He, Jesus, laid His life on the witness He could call in from the street—on you—on me. He laid His Kingdom right there—on you—on me.

A The first rays of the morning sun pierce the darkness. The rooster raises his head, stretches first one leg, then the other, and crows to greet the dawn.

Peter says it again. "I do not know the Man!" He says it a third time. "I am not one of His disciples!"

Again the rooster fills his lungs with the morning air, and the sound of his crowing fills the courtyard.

B And what about Jesus? He moves from judge to judge, from pillar to post, from scourging and crown to cross and nails.

Listen, as He prays out of the depths of His unconquerable love: "Father, forgive them." His prayer is not alone for the man with the hammer, or for the judges. His prayer is for the witnesses who didn't appear. Forgive them for they know not what they do.

Nor is that all. He moved into the damnation of the fearful Judge, into hell—for the witnesses that didn't come.

And when the pounding of hell was over, and His death was near, He raised His eyes to heaven and announced to the world, to the angels, and to His Father: "It is finished!" Forgiveness was there for Peter who denied, and for the witness who didn't show, and the soldier who smote Him, and for you—and for me.

A   Our Jesus is still on trial. He is endlessly accused by the world. Men still deride, ridicule, debase Him. He is still being judged.

The rays of the eternal day spear through the dark night of a sin-held world. The angel now, rather than the cock, stands poised to blast the trumpet.

The cry goes out. "Ask them which heard Me!" Ask John Doe to take the stand. Witness, are you ready?

B
> Can we whose souls are lighted
> With wisdom from on high,
> Can we to men benighted
> The lamp of life deny?
> Salvation! Oh, Salvation!
> The joyful sound proclaim
> Till each remotest nation
> Has learned Messiah's name.
> Amen.

A   The peace of God, which passes all understanding, keep our hearts and minds in faith in Christ Jesus—and ready to give answer to the call to take the stand whenever it comes. Amen.

V

"We Find Him Guilty"

2 Corinthians 1:9-10 (KJV)

A Dear and beloved ones,
"The Prisoner will rise and face the jury."

B He is not easy to look at, this Prisoner. If you are squeamish, turn away. There is a crown of thorns on His head. Those are not rubies dangling from it. They are drops of blood. His hands, bound now for hours, aching, swollen, pull His shoulders out of square. His clothing is torn and the thirty-nine lash marks show clearly.

Yet—whatever the pain—whatever the indignity—there is something about the bearing of the Prisoner—. He is not defeated.

A "Men of the jury, have you reached a verdict?"
"We have, your honor."
"Then let each man speak his finding."

B Your eyes move to the jury . . . from face to face. Every emotion is there, if not on one face, then on another. One has a kind of hellish glee. Another, refusing to look at the Prisoner, is marked by shame. Still another is proud, another frightened.

A There is a deadly silence in the courtroom. A Man's life hangs in the balance. One juror voting "INNOCENT" will free the Man. One vote!

B Caiaphas is first. With deliberate slowness he rises to his feet. With calculated intensity he eyes the Prisoner.

He shifts his high priest's robe from one arm to the other arm. The robe is torn from the neckline to the waist, and the ragged edges show quite clearly.

He speaks one word, sharp and clear in the stillness.

A   "Guilty!"

B   A soldier is next. He is given to snap judgments and quick decisions. Whatever facts are in, they are enough to determine the action.

His right hand makes a fist; as he slams it down into the open palm of his left hand, he speaks his word.

A   "Guilty!"

B   Next is Nicodemus. It is an obvious effort for him to stand. It is obviously even more difficult for him to speak. He pulls at a handkerchief, running the seam of it through his fingers. He looks long and hard at the Prisoner. He looks away. He wipes at the beads of perspiration on his forehead.

He is in an agony all his own.

His decision comes in a whisper.

A   "Guilty!"

B   Nicodemus sits and quietly weeps.

A   Herod has no problem. His hand and voice are steady. He's done this sort of thing before.

B   "Guilty!"

A   Judas rises. His face is absolutely impassive.

He had spent three years with Jesus. He heard Him; he saw Him; he knew Him. He had been with Him as recently as the Upper Room.

And all the while his mind had churned at fever pitch. But you couldn't tell it on his face.

B   "Guilty!"

A   The stillness of the room deepened. Unmistakably, it was Judas' voice, speaking in a desperate whisper.

"I have sinned in that I have betrayed innocent blood."

Yet, his vote was for the death penalty.

B   A citizen next.

He had sold his soul long ago for whatever there was to be

had. He lived by the "First me" philosophy, and the devil take the hindmost.

Even now his thumb rubbed the image of the emperor on the copper piece he clutched in his hand.

"Crucify Him."

A   Order! Order in the court! You are not to prescribe the penalty. Find you the Prisoner guilty or not?"

The citizen rubbed his copper piece.

B   "Guilty!" he said and sat down.

A   Satan was in the jury box.

He had been mulling over a thousand things.

There had been the wilderness experience, where he had been bested in the temptations he had offered the Prisoner.

There was a kingdom at stake. He was prince of it. He had endless rows of soldiers in it. He was in possession of countless numbers of souls in it. The only enemy that threatened his kingdom stood bound before him.

The decision was as simple as "Him or me" as far as he was concerned.

B   "Guilty!"

A   The decision of Barabbas was equally simple. He lived by the law of the jungle. He robbed and pillaged without compunction. He had been in a thousand scrapes and had gotten out of every one. This last one was close, but he had learned to give no quarter. With him it was winner take all. "Him or me?" Then there is no question.

B   "Guilty!"

A   Pilate's hands had been going through the motions of drying through the whole procedure. He put them under his arms to keep them still, only to forget himself and begin the drying pantomime all over.

He rose to make his statement. He put his hands behind his back, but even then he found himself rubbing them.

He looked for a moment as if he were about to make a qualifying statement. He paused, and then it came:

B "Guilty!"

A He sat down again. He folded his fingers together and held his hands tightly, so tightly his fingers ached. His eyes stared blankly as his thoughts went back—who knows where? To another trial? To Rome? To Law School? Slowly, yet once more, he dried his hands and slumped into his chair.

B A centurion next. He had learned obedience in the hard school of the army. He himself had hardened in the long course of his duty. His muscles bulged. His hand was calloused. But he had long ago learned to say "Yes, sir!" and like it or not do his appointed task. To refuse never entered his mind.

By what train of thinking beyond this he came to his verdict, it is impossible to tell. As crisply as if he were obeying an order, he rendered his judgment.

A "Guilty!"

B The Prisoner stood before the bench. Through the long and deadly recital He had not moved a muscle. He looked at each man as he made his pronouncement . . .

at Nicodemus for whom He had reached with tenderest care—

at Pontius Pilate, before whom He had spread the whole plan of salvation—

at the citizen, to whom He had given the wisdom and love of the heavenly Father . . .

and each one had found Him guilty. He looked at each man in turn. And each man lowered his eyes for what he saw in the eyes of the Prisoner.

A One more Juror to go.

One word will save Him. One "Innocent" will free Him. It is the last chance.

B The whole courtroom draws in its breath. The silence hangs more heavily on the courtroom air.

The Juror is God Himself!

Surely He will say the word to free.

A The Juror looks slowly around the courtroom. His eye rests briefly on His fellow jurors. His eyes move slowly around the courtroom. They rest for a moment on you and you.

They come at last to the Prisoner. They note the crown, the thorns, the lash welts, the bonds.

His mind races ahead to the punishment. To the cross. And beyond the cross to what must happen out there.

Each of His fellow jurors had reasons for his verdict. This Juror must have His reasons too. Yet how vastly different His than theirs!

B "Guilty!"

A The sentence of death was on Him!

B Guilty!

A The damnation of the world was upon Him!

B Guilty!

A Every man's hell was upon Him!

B Trust in God?

A The sentence of death was on Saul as he ploughed his way to Damascus. Jesus came to him on the hot and dusty road and took the sentence away.

We have the sentence of death in ourselves.

Our sins . . . our betrayals of the divine image . . . our berating of our brother . . . our rebellion . . . our pride . . . our very humanity . . .

    place the sentence of death upon us.

The Prisoner, the Son of God, Jesus, stood where indeed we ought to have stood . . .

    claimed by Satan's "Guilty" and
    condemned by our Lord's "Guilty."

Nothing could save us. Nothing!

B Nothing, that is, but God the Father's judgment from eternity on His Son.

Nothing, that is, but God the Father's "Guilty."

A It is Jesus who delivered us from so great a death.

It is the "Prisoner" who "doth deliver us" still.

B Let us pray

> Lamb of God, pure and holy,
> Who on the cross didst suffer,
> Ever patient and lowly,
> Thyself to scorn didst offer.
> All sins Thou borest for us,
> Else had despair reigned o'er us:
> Thy peace be with us,
> O Jesus! O Jesus!

A   Amen.

B   The peace of God, which passes all understanding, keep our hearts and minds in faith in Him who delivers us from so great a death, and in endless gratitude and unceasing praise. Amen.

VI

"Let the Punishment Fit the Crime"

Isaiah 53:6 (KJV)

A Dear and beloved ones,
   The Prisoner stands at the judgment bench.

   B The Prosecution had pressed His case and won.
   The defense had been most inadequate.
   The witnesses had been summoned and did not testify.
   Every man on the jury had found Him guilty.
   Justice must be done.

   A The situation is unique.
   The Judge is Father to the Prisoner; the Condemned is the only Son of His Father.
   The Father knows the total innocence of His Son. He has been an obedient Son in all things. He had accepted the task and completed it. In patience and persistence He had taught and loved and given and prayed for God's creatures. The Father knows, for heaven was never more concerned about the affairs of mankind than it was when the Son was servant on earth.
   The Father loves the Son. So great was His love that at least twice He had broken the silence of heaven to proclaim it. "This is My beloved Son, in whom I am well pleased," He had said.

   B The Prisoner stands silently before the Judge.
   The Son stands before the Father.

   A Perhaps the Son has been in error. The Prisoner may have been rash in the things He did, in the promises He made. We might well go back to look.
   He had done many rash things in the three years of His public life.

He had placed Himself between the throwers-of-stones and the woman caught in adultery.

He had hobnobbed with the despised tax collector, Matthew. He had been a repeated guest at the mansion of the usurer, Zaccheus.

After all, He had been seen with the wrong people. He had identified Himself with sinners.

As a man's actions condemn him, so do his words. Jesus was no different. His words helped place Him in this awkward position.

"Wherever and whenever you neglected a hungry child, or forgot an imprisoned man, or snubbed a cold and dying person, you were snubbing, or neglecting, or forgetting Me," He said.

The Son of Man has come into the world to save sinners," He said.

"Come unto Me, all ye that labor and are heavy laden, and I will give you rest," He said.

"Father, forgive them for they know not what they do," He said.

B   Every time He opened His mouth, every time He made a promise, every time He said a prayer . . . He identified Himself with sinners.

"All we like sheep have gone astray. We have gone every one his own way," the ancient prophet had said.

He identified with the sheep, though He was Shepherd.
He identified with man, though He was God.

A   His crime? He loved too much.

B   Now the Son stands before the Father.
Now the Accused stands before the Judge.

A   The situation is intensely unique.

B   Supposing you decided to intercede. You interrupt the proceedings to meet with the Judge on the Accused's behalf.
The Judge recesses the court to meet with you.

A   You tremble as you stand before Him.
"Does——He——have to die?!" you plead.

B   The Judge hesitates before He speaks. He looks long and hard at you. There is anger on His face, but there is love in His eyes.

His shoulders sag from the inner turmoil.

You thought the prayer scene in the Garden had been the deepest struggle, as the Savior pleaded with the Father. You sense now that there has been a deeper struggle still, raging in the heart of the Father.

A   "Do you know the punishment for sin?" He asked slowly and with awesome effort.

You reply, "To tell the truth I haven't thought too much about sin or its consequences."

"Let Me, then, see if I can make you realize what it is.

   Sin is rebellion against God.

    Sin is treason against God.

     Sin is defiance against Me.

      Sin is a wall you build to shut Me out.

"I had plans for you. Dreams you could never comprehend. I thought of a world of peace, of men living together as one great family. I asked for kindness and love between all people. I created a heaven for you, so glorious that imagination and the words you use cannot touch the splendor of it.

"I have loved you with a love beyond grasping.

"And you defied Me, O man. You rebelled against My will and against My love.

"Now the punishment must fit the crime. Now the judgment must meet the sin.

"The judgment must be without mercy. Were it you, O sinner, standing before the bar out there, I would condemn you to eternal hell!

"I would jam open the doors of hell, so that you would forever see the glory of heaven—but I would build no bridge over the great gulf between hell and heaven.

"I banish the sinner out beyond My love, eternally."

B   He pauses.

You tremble. You speak . . . a whisper . . . no more:

   "God be merciful to me."

A   He continues now. Tired. Drained. Yet having to go on and through what lies ahead.

"You pray for mercy, sinful man. I will give you mercy. Let us go back into the courtroom."

B   The Prisoner stands at the judgment bench still.
The Father confronts the Son.

A   "You have at My will identified Yourself with sinful man, O My Son. You have taken to Yourself the world's sins. And because You have taken the iniquity of all mankind upon Yourself, I cannot but see in You the defiance, the rebellion, of all humanity.

"Though You are innocent of the crime of man's sins . . .
    I find You guilty
    and demand the full penalty of the law.
"The law clearly states that the wages of sin is death. It allows no quarter, for the soul that sins must die."

B   The Judge has difficulty breathing. You cannot tell if His face has anger in it; it does have determination. You sense something else about Him . . . a sorrow too deep for words . . . a hurt too deep for tears . . .

    "I find You guilty of mankind's sin;
    I condemn You to hell!"

A   The Judge turned quickly, lest He see the Prisoner's face. He left the courtroom immediately, closing the door behind Him.

Centurion guards roughly took the Prisoner from the room.
The jury filed out, not speaking.
The spectators, appalled by the decision of the court and the sentence of the Judge, left quietly.

B   You alone remain behind.
You must have time to think.
You go over the trial . . . the weak defense . . . the Prosecution . . . the jury . . .
How does it all make sense? What's the key? Where's the answer?

A Then slowly in the quietness, the answer comes. A tear rolls down your cheek.

You are the key to it all.

You are the sinner . . . often defiant . . . perverse.

Jesus is the key to it all.

He was willing . . . obedient unto death . . . even the death of the cross.

Love is the key to it all.

God the Father, willing, in love, to offer His Son . . . to condemn His Son.

B For you! For you He laid on Him the iniquity of us all.

A Faith is the key to it all.

Faith that accepts His substitution for you.

B In the darkness you whisper . . .

"Lord, I believe—help Thou mine unbelief."

Then, with such knowledge, and in faith, you rise from your knees, and go out into the sunlight.

A We'll think upon Thy mercy without ceasing,
That earth's vain joys to us no more be pleasing;
To do Thy will shall be my sole endeavor
Henceforth forever.
And when, dear Lord, before Thy throne in heaven
To us the crown of joy at last is given,
Where sweetest hymns Thy saints forever raise Thee,
We, too, shall praise Thee. Amen.

B The peace of God, which passes all understanding, keep your hearts and minds in faith in our gracious and glorious Lord Jesus, and your life in the endless sunshine of His love. Amen.

Cross Sermons

Cross Section

Luke 3:21-22 (RSV)

When you want to sin, you must get rid of the First Table of the Law. To state it more concretely, if you want to sin you must first get rid of God. Or, if you are involved in sin, it means you have already committed the first sin which is to smash the First Table of the Law. Once being free of the First Table it is of no consequence to you what transpires in relation to the Second Table. If you get rid of God, the world is your "oyster," as the saying is.

Cross Section
THE WORLD

Moses' forty days in the holy mountain proved too long for Israel waiting at the mountain's foot. It didn't matter to them that they were no longer slaves, that a pillar of fire had led them through the barren reaches of the desert wasteland, or that Pharaoh's charioteers had perished in the mighty miracle of the parted sea. The word was out. "Moses (and his God) is dead, perished in the mountain. Let's make us a god of our own devising." Smash went the First Table of the Law! Aaron fashioned a golden calf-god for them. They danced before it. They sang hymns to it. No doubt they prayed to it. "Yahweh-God died with Moses," they said. All the historians and all the artists paint the scene about the golden calf as one huge debauchery, which is probably what happened. With the smashing of the First, the Second Table of the Law was smashed, too.

Moses and Joshua returning from the camp bearing the Law engraved on stone by the finger of God Himself, heard the boisterous worship. Moses' "anger burned hot." He threw the stone tables to the ground. They broke into a thousand pieces. His action truly dramatized the terrible abomination by Yahweh's own and chosen people. The truth is, the Law was broken before Moses ever left the mountain top.

Israel and her golden calf is symbol for the world and its dumb idols through all the history of humanity. When the Holy Spirit uses that word "world," He puts His own meaning into it. The "world" for Him is humanity in rebellion against God.

More space is given by the Holy Spirit to describe rebellious humanity than to retell the story of how it was redeemed. The historical books, many of the Psalms, and the prophets tell and retell of man's wickedness. In Romans Paul with constrained brushstrokes paints the golden calf scene as it happened in his day. "And since they did not see fit to acknowledge God, God gave them up to a base mind and to improper conduct. . . . Though they know God's decree that those who do such things deserve to die, they not only do them but approve those who practice them" (Romans 1:18-32).

Not to belabor the point, but this day is no improvement. However this generation has achieved it, the First Table of the Law lies smashed again at the foot of the holy mountain! With God tucked away in a safe corner, or, for many, dead and buried, this generation has gone on to ravish and smash the Second Table. Down with authority! Down with integrity! Down with institutions of all kinds! Down with mores and morality and noble ethics! Down with the other person; I come first. My satisfaction—my pleasure—my freedom. Murders are now wholesale. Marriage, who needs it!? So what's the matter with swinging and what's the matter with gay and what's the matter with stealing? And what's the matter with conniving?

Joseph, servant lad in Potiphar's house in Egypt, was invited into bed by Potiphar's wife. The prospect may have been tempting, but Joseph remembered the First Table of the Law. "How can I do this wickedness and sin against God?" he said, and paid honor to the Second Table.

It is the idolatrous, rebellious, murderous, adulterous, greedy, conniving world that God loved enough to send His Son to redeem it. It is this human family, which disgraces the Creator's world, defies the Creator's existence and denies His will, and smashes the Tables of the Law continuously—it is this human family that God loves.

Cross Section
GOD

There was an enormous problem and dilemma in the heart of God. He is a just and righteous God. His "In the day that thou sinnest thou shalt surely die" could not be revoked. "The wages of sin is death." "By one man sin entered the world, and death by sin." God does not change. He is just. He is righteous. He is a sin-hating God.

The love/justice dilemma was resolved in the person of Christ, Son of the living God. He would be the place where justice and love would meet. In love He would take into His own soul the righteous wrath of God against sin. He would be the Propitiation for the rebellious world.

Cross Section
JESUS

That is why on a certain day down at the Jordan River where the people were being baptized by the prophet John, Jesus of Nazareth also was baptized. Then as the ritual ended, Jesus prayed. A phenomenon occurred. First a dove, identified by St. Luke as the Holy Spirit, appeared and descended upon Him. And out of the heavens a voice, heard by those who were present, spoke to Jesus: "You are My beloved Son; with You I am well pleased." It was God the Father speaking, commissioning Him to redeem the world.

Whatever the little boy Jesus thought when His parents told Him about His birth, or whatever may have been going through His mind as a twelve-year-old in the temple discoursing with the doctors in the temple, in this moment of His baptism, there was laid upon Him the responsibility to redeem the world. If He understood it before, then He knew that now God's hour had come. If He didn't know it before, now He did. Do not minimize the Father's involvement, for the Christ-commissioning would cost Him indescribable agony when the inevitable cross held the Christ captive a few years down the path of history. The Spirit was at the baptism for He is charged with giving power to the Word. In a little while He will lead Jesus into the wilderness school and allow Him to be sorely tempted by Satan. He will retire into the shadows in which God dwells until on Pentecost He will burst upon the earth to build and adorn the Kingdom of Grace.

The whole plan of God staggers and defies the imagination. Jesus, who is the Christ, starts out alone against all the forces of evil, against rebellious mankind with all its sickening sins, against the human family that will demand His life, against the wrath of His righteous Father. The line stretches from His baptism to the cross. He will walk the narrow line, never deviating from it. This is His mission. This is His destiny. This is the world's salvation. This is our salvation. Not once did He hesitate on His journey downward to the cross and death.

Cross Section
US

Jesus commissioned His disciples: "Go and preach the Gospel and baptize all people in the name of the Father and the Son and the Holy Spirit." His disciples have been doing that since first He commissioned them. We are a baptized people. St. Paul claims, under the Holy Spirit: "We are buried with Christ by baptism into death." God telescopes us into the very death and resurrection of Jesus. In baptism His death for the remission of sins becomes ours, too. In Christ the Father sees us, and frees us from the weight of judgment against us. Our baptism is our authentication that we are His.

If you do a cross section on our baptism you will find striking things going on in the simple yet profound Sacrament. By the waters of regeneration we are snatched from the family of Adam to live in the family of God! The theologians call it the forgiveness of sin, including the removal of our hereditary guilt. By our baptism we are transplanted into the body of Christ. There we are nourished in the holy Word. We become a functioning part of the body, making our contribution to it from it. We are ordained to the royal priesthood. Suddenly in the cross section there is evidence of a parallelism. As Christ was sent to the world at His baptism, so we by our baptism are sent to the rebellious, sinful mankind, too.

46

We, by our baptism and commitment to Christ, are to be in the world, but not of it. We, in Christ, have a newness of life, a renewing of our minds. We are commissioned to be "lights" and "cities on a hill" to the world. We are to be God's "letter" to the world. Because of our love for Christ, who first loved us, we are honest when the world is deceitful; we love when the world hates; we are morally clean when the world fornicates; we are content when the world connives; we serve when the world is greedy, we give when the world demands. How else can we be the salt of the earth? How else can we requite the love given us so generously?

As Christ bore witness to the Father, we by our baptism give witness to Christ and His Father. "How can they believe in Him of whom they have not heard? How can they hear without a preacher?" The most eloquent sermons are not those preached from the church's pulpits. They are the quiet words you say to the world about Jesus who reigns as Lord, Jesus who loves, Jesus who wants all the human family in His kingdom of grace and glory.

Christ was baptized, and in His baptism He was commissioned to the cross. We are baptized and must daily drown the Old Adam in us, that is, we must die again and again to what we are in Adam, and by the renewing of our minds, we must be what we are called to be in Christ, our Lord.

Amen.

Cross Out: Cross In

Luke 4:1-13 (RSV)

Dear Friends,

According to those who have been there, fasting as a spontaneous act of self-denial follows a fairly certain and predictable course. First, they report, one feels the lack of nourishment, but in a while the desire for food vanishes. The body begins to live on its own stored-up calories. When the vital organs are attacked, however, there is a wild, elemental hunger. Once this has passed a psychic process sets in. The body becomes more supple, the spirit grows freer. At last the soul stands stripped, open to all forces that may play against it. There is a general vertigo of the spirit. At this point there is great danger, for the very soul can move into crisis. Some feel that this is the formula through which Jesus worked in the wilderness. As vertigo set in, Satan, antagonist to Christ, moved in to seduce Him from His divine mission.

Others feel that the temptations are a veritable psychological gold mine. Man begins life with a desire for food, basic and elemental. As he grows older he has a thirst for power and position. There comes a time, if circumstances are right, when he feels himself a god. Satan, it is said, addressed his temptations of Christ to the psychological ages of man. Where the psychologist would take the account from there is anyone's guess.

Cross In

Always there is drive and purpose and point in the life of Jesus. The evangelists will not let the cross out of their sight, for they know that Jesus must fix His eyes on it, and walk the narrow road to it. St. Luke, himself under the power of the Holy Spirit, carefully calls our attention to the Spirit's guiding in

Jesus' life. It is Luke who told how the blessed virgin mother bowed her head before Gabriel and asked how it could be that she should be unwed yet bear a son. And the angel said to her: "The Holy Spirit will come upon you, and the power of the Most High will overshadow you; therefore the Child to be born will be called holy, the Son of God." The Spirit was there in that most profound moment in history when the Son left Glory to become Jesus on our earth.

At the moment of the announcement of His mission to Jesus, all that were gathered on the Jordan bank with Him witnessed the Spirit in the form of a dove. Did the Spirit's presence convince Jesus of the enormity of the truth about Himself He hadn't dared to dwell on before this hour? The Spirit filled Jesus as He turned from the Jordan, and the Spirit led Him (Mark says "drove Him") into the wilderness until the struggle about His personhood and mission were resolved. (Incidentally, when the temptations were over, it it was in the power of the Spirit that Jesus journeyed to Galilee and began to teach in the synagogues there.)

From the baptism to the wilderness experience is not so very far. Ringing in Jesus' heart and head is the enormous question, "If I am the Son of God—If I am the Son of God—If I am the Son of God—What does that mean? What does that mean to Me?" The problem was enormously perplexing. He wrestled with the question. He prayed. The Holy Spirit must surely have been in His struggle. Gradually, an answer emerged. (Granted, any answer our human reason might deduce can be faulty.) He was on mission of the Father, who had so tenderly addressed Him at His baptism. If He is Son, then He must be obedient to His Father's will. The Father's will required the cross. He would be "obedient unto death, even the death of the cross." The struggle to understanding ended at last. It had taken 40 days. He was at the point of exhaustion, but He was convinced. The cross was in!

Cross Out?

"Then cometh the devil."

Precisely at the point of struggle, with the same logic and attack with which he had seduced Adam and Eve, the devil tempted Him. "If You are the Son of God, turn these stones to bread and eat!" "One simple miracle, Jesus. It will solve Your hunger problem. It will solve a bigger problem—Are You truly the Son of God?" Proof just now of His Sonship would have been welcome, but faith and trust and commitment do not need proof. "It is written: Man shall not live by bread alone." Too bad, Satan, that you were deprived of your free will when you fell, for the Holy Spirit who convinces by the Word, might by this Word have persuaded you. The cross was in!

Then to a high place, and the devil showed Jesus a panoramic view of all authorities and their glory. "This," he said, "I will give You for a single bend of Your knee before me." For a moment the cross loomed between Jesus and the Kingdom He would one day rule. With the cross the redemption of the world in rebellion against His Father flashed before Him. The Son, obedient to the Father's will, brought His life again into focus. "It is written," He said, "You shall worship the Lord your God!" The cross was in!

Once again, high on a temple tower, temptation to seduction came to Jesus. "If You are the Son of God, throw Yourself down from here. Your Father's angels will have charge over You and guard You. Have You tested Your Father-Son relationship, Jesus of Nazareth? Do You really believe You are God's Son? Put the Father to the test." Once again, with Scripture, Jesus drove the devil away from Him. "It is said, you shall not tempt the Lord your God."

Cross In

Satan left. Luke bids us watch for his return, for he will seek the opportune time to come back. The cross is in; Satan wants it out!

When the temptations were done, Jesus had no proof that He had the power of God. A miracle with the stones would have reassured Him but it would also have robbed Him of His faith and destroyed His commitment. He had no evidence of His own authority. Weak from hunger, exhausted from the temptations, He moved as the carpenter's son to His mission. He had remained faithful to His calling there on the mountain top in the second recorded attempt to seduce Him from His course. He had no in-depth, firsthand knowledge of the Father's concern for

Him. But He had learned the Father's will there in the wilds about the Jordan. If that will included death in Jerusalem, He would be faithful to the Father's trust. The cross was in.

St. Peter sees Satan stalking his prey like a roaring lion. We who are baptized into the Kingdom of God, we who have by the power of the Spirit committed ourselves to Christ, we to whom the cross is in, are Satan's prey.

Cross Out

Crossing out the cross from our lives saves us from a multitude of problems. Without the cross, the sky's the limit. We are free of all restraints, save those imposed by civil law, if we cannot skirt them. No cross in our lives. Satan has no cause to worry about us. No Christ in our hearts, and Satan breathes free. Curse and swear and lie—that's all right. Forget the Word, neglect the gathering of Christ's people—that's all right! Rebellion? Okay! Hate and murder! Fine. Sex without restraint? Who will care! Greed? Usury? Selfishness? Fine. God? If there is a God, where is He? With the cross out of a person's heart, the whole gamut of evil which proceeds from the unregenerate heart is free to gush out.

Cross In

But if the cross is in our lives, that is, if Christ is in us and we are in Christ, the story must be exceedingly different. The person in Christ is a new creature. The cross in his heart becomes the symbol par excellence of the great love of God and of His Son by which he aspires and by which he lives. The regenerate heart produces the fruits of the Spirit—that same Spirit that led Christ into the wilderness, that filled Him, that put power to believe into His words—produces love, joy, peace.

But the cross in our hearts makes us fair game for Satan until at last he is cast into the bottomless pit. We can be sure that temptations will be ever with us, for Satan is tireless and exceedingly persistent. At every point where the mighty affirmation stands, Satan comes with his doubt-producing insinuations. "Jesus Christ is Lord? That big Policeman? That fearful Judge? What God? Thou shalt love thy neighbor as thyself? You mean those people down the street? You mean them Japs? You mean whitey? Keep thyself pure? Dope doesn't hurt; illicit sex is more fun; you mean I can't think any more? Go, speak the Gospel to every creature! There he is, send him, send him. Give as the Lord has prospered you! You don't really mean a percentage? Every week?"

Like the Pharisee at prayer in a Jesus-parable, we seek to justify ourselves and what we do. "That's the way I am!" "He hit me first!" "My parents." "My childhood." "My culture." "Everybody does it." "It's my life." Things like that we say to ourselves (and sometimes to God), and do our Old Adam thing. Cross out! Satan in!

Again, the cross in our hearts is our one defense against Satan and his temptation to despair and other great shame and vice. If we stumble, if in our perverse way we entertain Satan's line of argument, the Christ in our hearts brings comfort and relief when we return to Him. For the relief that He alone can give, Christ set His face to the cross in obedience to the Father's will, and moved steadily down the rugged way to do it. At the cross we begin our journey to the crown of life. Would that our commitment to the crown matched Christ's commitment to our cross.

Amen.

Cross Purposes

Luke 5:18-26 (RSV)

Do you remember those neat plastic overlays in the medical books? Do they still have them? The first overlay revealed the human body; flip a page and the muscular system is revealed; another page and there's the vascular system, or the digestive system or the nervous system, until finally only the skeleton is left. Those overlays suggest a good way to look at miracles.

The miracle of the palsied man, for instance, has for first overlay the outward circumstances of the event. The house is crowded; Jesus is inside; a palsied man needs healing; his friends let him down through an opening in the roof, right in front of Jesus. The whole idea was ingenious. The sick man's friends maneuvered him up the outside stairway to the rooftop and then let him down, on his pallet, through the opening. They blocked out the light for the room below, of course. Conversation stopped while the maneuvering went on. Slowly the pallet descended. The light flooded into the room again. The framework for the action had been set.

Flip an overleaf. Jesus of Nazareth replaces the men, the man, and the pallet. He looks no different from any other man in the room. His hands are slightly gnarled from His years of carpentering. His parentage is two peasants from Nazareth. He has had some notoriety. A few healings have been attributed to Him and He holds your attention with His stories and seems to speak with authority.

Jesus speaks. "Man, your sins are forgiven."

Cross Purposes I

Time to flip another overleaf. The Pharisees are aghast. God alone forgives sins. Who does this peasant think He is? Healing we can understand; others have had the power. But forgiving sins! The man speaks blasphemy. There is immediate tension in the room. Obviously the Pharisees and Jesus are at cross purposes.

Turn another overleaf. The picture is Jesus again. Now He is revealed as the Son of Man with authority to forgive sins. "Take up your bed and walk," He said to the palsied man. And the man promptly was healed, arose from the pallet, gathered the ropes into the blanket, rolled it all up and, with light step, left the house and went to his own home.

The next overleaf shows the "miracle system." The miracles of Jesus are in themselves a fascinating study. There is hardly room for more than a passing note about them just now. Suffice it to say that though they demonstrate the power of God, much more than that they are signs that point to Jesus, Son of Man. They gather about the cross and each in its own way becomes a signpost pointing to that greatest of all signs, the redeeming cross of Jesus.

So we have come to the last page lying beneath or behind all the overleaves, the skeleton, as it were, for the miracles, for the Gospels, for Jesus. Do you see it just here? It is the Roman execution tree, invented by the heinous mind of man and chosen by God to be the instrument of Christ's death. You can put the pages back now—Christ as the Son of Man—the flabbergasted Pharisees—Jesus of Nazareth—the specific miracle. Now you know that behind them stands the supporting beam, the skeleton on which this and a hundred other stories in the Gospels hang.

Some things we just have to understand. Jesus was commissioned to redeem the world in the preworld councils of the Trinity. He was "ordained" to the task in the waters of the Jordan. In the wilderness retreat, through prayer and fasting and waiting on His Father, He fought through the meaning of Sonship and its call to obedience. If the Father's will required His life on the cross at Calvary, so be it—He would be obedient to the cross.

Cross Purposes II

In that crowded room where the healing miracle happened, Jesus, for the sake of the nameless man, renewed His commitment to the Father, to the cross, and to us. He knew and acknowledged the purpose of His life; He understood the purposes of the cross. He fully comprehended what was involved in the healing of this man or a thousand other people. He was borrowing forgiveness against the payment of the penalty. Jesus had such a marvelous way of loving. About the time they had raised the cross, dropped it into its socket, and driven stakes to hold it firm, Jesus prayed His great prayer for their forgiveness. Oh, not just for the soldiers and the mockers there on the hill, but for all the generations that preceded Him and for all the generations to come so long as the world should stand. "Father," He prayed, "forgive them. They know not what they do."

He had five choices in the Greek for the term "to forgive." He chose the one that begs that the judgment be postponed, that the sentence not be put into effect at once. He prayed that God would not put the storms of judgment into motion, not until after the salvation of the world was effected, not until He had made good His promise to the palsied man, and Moses, and Elijah. Not until He had redeemed Caiaphas, Peter, Pilate, His mother, the men with their railing voices, and the soldiers with their hammers. "Hold back Your wrath from them, O My Father, until I shall have redeemed them and they have opportunity to repent and believe."

The prayer, by the nature of the great High Priest who prayed there and the great High Priest who offered Himself there, reached forward from the cross as well. It reached through the 1st century and sustained John on the Isle of Patmos, into the 16th to sustain Luther and Zwingli, into the 20th to touch the lives of natives in far-off corners of the globe, and even into your life, sinner, friend, redeemed. "Father, forgive Joan and John, for they know not what they do." Wondrous strange and strangely wonderful, that the world has moved far through the 20th century because of a prayer sent heavenward by the dying Christ. Never, dear friend, underestimate the power and the purpose of Christ's cross.

So very many people are at cross-purposes with Christ. The Pharisees and teachers of the law in the crowded house in Galilee were at cross-purposes with Him. They saw the miracle and accepted it. What a wonder this Jesus is! They heard Him forgive the man's sins, but they failed to see the Christ behind it. For them the sign pointed to the carpenter's Son, and if it pointed beyond they never noticed. Many people, like Demas, are entranced by Jesus, the Miracle Worker, but, like the Pharisees, miss the Christ behind the miracle and the story. Pray God you have turned the overlays to discover the cross behind the event and behind the deed, the Doer. If you have, quietly slip to your knees and offer the sacrifice of praise and thanksgiving!

If forgiveness and reconciliation with the Father were the cross purposes then, what are the cross purposes for us who live by the sign of the cross now? Its purposes are, first of all, to free us, as St. Paul writes to the Romans, from the wrath of God against our sins. To free us from the pressure of the Law which drives us to the ground in dark despair in our inability to live by it, to free us from sin, and to free us from the terror of death. "Father, forgive them while I take Your wrath into My body, and their sins, and the consequences of the Law, and the specter of the end. Let Me free them from these things." No wonder the soul of the Christian soars and sings. He is free of crushing, damning legislation.

In no way is freedom to be license. We are not freed from bondage in order to sin. We dare not flaunt back at God a misunderstanding of His unspeakable gift to us. If you do not know what to do with your freedom, ask Him. He has wisdom for you in His holy Word. Husbands, love your wives; wives, love your husbands! Children, honor your parents; parents, be patient with your children! Blessed are the meek, the poor in spirit, the humble! The Son of Man came not to be ministered unto, but to minister! I have washed your feet as an example! Bless them that curse you, bless and curse not! Ye shall be witnesses to Me!

But chief among all the things that you might do, certainly, is to do what the man did as he picked up his bed, and left the house, forgiven, healed—he glorified God. Perhaps he saw the Christ and the cross behind the miracle! The Pharisees, too, glorified God and they were filled with awe. Did they suspect that behind the Jesus-overlay was indeed the very Son of God?

They had trouble knowing what to make of it all and Luke says that they said as much: "We have seen strange things today!"

Is there a better word for us to say, knowing the story behind forgiveness, understanding the holy purposes of the cross, and hearing the Savior's prayer that brought the dawn today (Father, hold back the judgment), and knowing that in Him we are free to serve the living God? "We have seen strange things today." Accept our trembling praise, O Lord.

Amen.

Cross Words

Luke 9:34-36 (RSV)

Martin Buber, Israeli theologian and philosopher, did a piece he called "I and Thou," suggesting by adaptation some principles for Christians. We must be in the love relationship, the "I—Thou," as demanded by the ancient law, "Thou shalt love thy neighbor as thyself." The "I—Thou" relationship can be one of hate. It is possible to be in an "I—It" relationship, that is, a relationship of indifference. (We have such relationships with newspaper boys and waitresses. We may have such a relationship with other members of the community of faithful!) The hate relationship is, in a sense, preferable to the relationship of indifference—for hate is between people, indifference between a person and a "thing."

The ultimate relationship of the creature is relationship with the Creator. Here man's true identity reaches the "I and Thou" heights the Creator planned for him from the beginning. It is the Christian understanding and faith that the "I" and the "Thou" require a "He" between them, for sin has come into the world breaking the "I—God" relationship. "He" is Christ, who by substitution for me, suffered my damnation and entered my hell that I might be reconciled to God. The formula "I—He—Thou, Me—Christ—the Father" is basic to grasping the whole New Testament concept. The formula might be otherwise stated: "The Sinner—Redeemed by Christ—enters into the joy of the Father." "Confession—forgiveness in Christ—reconciliation with God." The "I—Thou" relationship with God is made possible only through Jesus, the Christ. It is always amazing to me that such small words can be freighted with such enormous significance: "I—He—Thou"!

There are many significant facts in the Transfiguration text, most of which we cannot follow this morning for lack of time.

Besides, we are dedicated to watch Christ move toward the cross on these Sundays in Lent, and it would be against the rules we have set for ourselves to follow another line of thinking. Knowing that we are not doing justice to the exciting Transfiguration account, let us pick those words which open the window on the road to the cross a little wider, for we are concerned about the high price of reconciliation. Damnation, after all, is free. Redemption required the damnation of Christ, the Son of God.

> Ye who think of sin but lightly
> Nor suppose the evil great
> Here may view its nature rightly,
> Here its guilt may estimate.
> Mark the Sacrifice appointed,
> See who bears the awful load;
> 'Tis the WORD, the LORD'S ANOINTED,
> Son of Man and Son of God.

The Event

On the mountain of Transfiguration Christ appeared for a moment in dazzling glory. Moses and Elijah, the giver and the enforcer of the ancient Law, broke from the barrier of invisibility which hides heaven from our curiosity, and for a little spell spoke—in casual conversation—with Jesus. Their conversation concerned His death at Jerusalem (Christ you see, is given no relief from the cross which stands at the end of His life). The Father is not involved in the conversation. Two of the saints in glory break the barrier, but the Father is silent. The Son, who has left glory for the redemption of the human family, who has the privilege of the Father's house, is denied entrance. Heaven comes to Him. After a little time, the two great saints departed and returned to their place and part in glory.

Peter, of course, was ecstatic. His mile-a-minute mind had a plan before the saints had disappeared. He might better have taken a little time to think what the conversation meant, but all he could think of was to stay on the mountain top, make "booths" for the two saints and Jesus, and bask with the others in the glory of this unsustainable moment.

Then the voice.

Cross Words: I—Thou

God, who had spoken out of a cloud at Christ's baptism, speaks again. "Thou art My Son," the Father had said then. The "I—Thou" relation, the Father is "I," the Son is "Thou." It is almost profane to speak of the love between the Father and the Son, for who (except in human terms) can understand their relationship? "You are My beloved Son!" The echoes of that relationship pulsate through the Christ biographies. Repeatedly He was alone in prayer with His Father. His high priestly prayer (John 17) vibrates with the unity of the Father and the Christ. "I and My Father are One." "That the love with which Thou hast loved Me may be in them, and I in them." Even the cross could not break the profound union of Christ with His Father. "Father, forgive!" "Father, into Thy hands I commend My spirit."

But there was that terrifying and terrified cry from the dark cloud covering the cross to the Father on His throne: "My God, My God, why hast Thou forsaken Me!" Do you want to understand something about that cross word? Draw a line, then, from the cross and the Christ it held, not by nails, but by the Son's obedience, to the mountain of Transfiguration, where the Father speaks a second time from the clouds. The disciples—and Jesus—hear His words.

Cross Words: I—It

"This is My Son, My Chosen." This is not conversation between the Father and the Son on Transfiguration Hill. There is a switch in pronouns when the Father speaks. Christ, who sees God's whole Plan of redemption, who thinks the whole Plan and lives in the whole Plan, hears the "This." It sears His soul. "The Father has, here in the moment when I have been given a glimpse of heaven, begun the terrible process of redemption. He has taken a step back from Me. He has nothing to say to Me. He speaks to the disciples and I have become "This," not "Thou," to Him. The first tear, the first flash of insight into the Passion, happened in the Father's careful choice of words. Christ heard and Christ knew.

The Christ biographies hold other clues to this terrible separation of the divine "I—Thou." Follow along the line from the Transfiguration to the cross. In Gethsemane Jesus, our Lord, prayed with a great agony. "Father remove the cup; but Your will be done." He prayed and prayed and prayed. Blood dropped in great drops from His forehead to the dust. When He said His Amen at last an angel appeared "to strengthen Him." The Father didn't come to put His arm around the Son. There was no voice from heaven to reassure Him. Just an angel messenger with a message. "The Father says, 'No!'"

A moment or two down the line Jesus hangs pinioned to the cross. A cloud covered Crucifixion Hill. "It's an eclipse," the astronomers said. "It's a cold front blowing through," the weather people said. "There's a storm coming," the housewives said. They were all wrong. "God has shut out His Son," the Spirit says. "The Son of God was in hell," the forgiven sinner says. The great, forbidding cloud was there for three hours. Under it, Christ is in hell. From the darkness, out of His cloud, He calls to heaven at the last, "My God, My God, why hast Thou forsaken Me?"

Cross Words: I—Thou

Since the fall in Eden, with the presence of sin in the world, there is only one way to come at last into glory. Only one way—and that way includes hell. No man, no woman, would ever stand in glory who had to walk the path through hell—not one. Who can stand against the wrath of God? Who, being caught by Satan in hell, can escape? There is *no one*. No one, that is, but Christ. The statement, since the cross, can be reframed. There is only one way to glory. Hell has been eliminated from the Way there. Christ is the Way. One goes to the Father only through Him.

Since the cross words were spoken, Christ stands forever between the "I" of the sinner and the "Thou" of God. The great words of the faith draw Christ into their very heart. Words like expiation, propitiation, justification, reconciliation, redemption, mercy, grace, and forgiveness reach, each in its own way, to my "I" and God's "Thou." The formula is indeed "I—Christ—Thou."

Good people of God! The relationship that God has established with you through Christ is a noble pattern for you to emulate in your relationship with the members of your community. You can, you ought to have an "I—Thou" relationship with every person gathered here to worship God this day. Look at each person through the eyes of Jesus; behold how Jesus loves him or her! You can, you must see Jesus in the other person, for Jesus surely identifies Himself with each of us. The relationship is the same "I, Fred—Jesus Christ—Thou, John!" Remember what they said about the early community? "Behold how they love each other!"

Beyond the community the problem becomes more difficult, but we are called upon to strive for the same "I—Thou" relationship. Never ought we to let the relationship deteriorate to "I—It," for to do so is to forget and to betray our Christ. Between "me and my enemy" we must place the Christ, and love him until he becomes for us at least a "Thou." "It's hard," you say. The way of the cross was never meant to be easy—for Jesus or for His disciples! The end of the way is to see the risen and reigning Christ. It is to behold the radiant splendor of the Father's face. It is to thrill to the person of the Holy Spirit, who led us into faith and who sets us on the Way. Christ thought the way to the cross and beyond worth all the effort for us. We ought do no less for Him and every peer.

Amen.

FIFTH SUNDAY IN LENT

Cross Examination

Luke 9:18-22 (RSV)

Dear Christian Friends,

Sometimes there are questions, but we can't find the answers. Sometimes answers are available, but the questions can't be found. For instance, the answer might be "12," but the nature of the answer allows endless questions. Is the right one, "What do 6 and 6 total?" Is it, "How many disciples did Jesus have?" Is it, "In which number is the symbolism of our Lord's relation to the earth expressed?" The exercise appears futile, even though the process must continually go on.

One of the old nursery rhymes deals with the problem. Cock Robin is dead! That's the answer. Now the questions have to come: "How did Cock Robin die?" "Who killed Cock Robin?" "Did you kill Cock Robin?" At last the right question leads to the culprit. "I," said the sparrow, "with my bow and arrow, I killed Cock Robin!" The old rhyme begs a deeper question, out of history. "What historical person does Cock Robin represent?" That's the real question in the case.

The search for proper answers in a court of law calls for examination of the accused and the witnesses. In the form of questions and answers the prosecution and defense lawyers search out the facts in the case. The privilege of examination and cross-examination is given to both sides. Questions and answers and more questions, on and on as long as the search for truth requires it.

Examination—Cross-Examination

In our text Jesus has a question for the disciples. He is searching for an answer; the first question was preparatory for the one that follows it.

Q. "Who do people say that I am?"

There is more to the question than meets the eye. Jesus is inquiring into His effectiveness as a communicator. Have men grasped the significance of His sermons? Have they understood His parables? Do they see behind His daily signs? Has the Messiah-fact, the Christ-truth, gotten through to them? Will anybody be saved from perdition by what He has so far done or said, or hoped or prayed? The answer is not encouraging.

A. John the Baptist; but others say, Elijah; and others, that one of the old prophets has risen.

Current among the teachers in the time of Jesus was a concept that one day one of the great prophets would return. It could be that Moses would somehow return to life, not necessarily transmigrated, but "somehow" he would return. He would restate the great old Mosaic laws. If Moses himself would not be sent, then another of the prophets would come. Candidates for the "return to life" were Jeremiah, Elijah, or some other of the prophets. Apparently John the Baptist, beheaded within the last year, had become a possible candidate for "return." Had he not sounded like Moses of old? It may have been a tribute to Jesus that people felt that way about Him, but it was hardly the answer to the question Jesus wanted. But then, not everyone in Palestine had heard Jesus speak as often or had seen so many miracles as the disciples. Perhaps the question was unfair, and the answer what was to be expected. A second question was in order.

Q. "Who say you that I am?"

A. "The Christ of God!"

It was Simon Peter who answered. Behind the miracles, in the authoritative words, from the voice out of the clouds, at the mountaintop prayers, Simon had discovered the awesome truth. The Messiah had come into the world. The Christ was here—in their very midst. Peter (and probably most of the other disciples) had moved step by step toward understanding this strange and wonderful Man. They had been able to brush aside the current and popular beliefs that the promised Messiah would come in a blaze of glory. (Satan had suggested that He should with the temptation to jump from the temple parapet.) He had come quietly instead. He had revealed His identity slowly. Peter, with insights given him by heaven, had a ready

64

answer. Here was the Fulfiller of prophecy, whose arrival had been announced in Eden, whose certainty was promised to Abraham; the Servant of whom Isaiah wrote to comfort the people in Babylon, the One who should establish the new covenant with God. Here in the person of Jesus was the Messiah, "the Christ of God!"

Hypothetical Cross-Examination

As St. Luke ferreted out the story from those whom he questioned about Jesus in order to write his Gospel, he learned that Jesus commanded them to say nothing about their blessed insight. He would go on preaching, defining the Kingdom with parables, revealing the Father, and loving the unlovable. Perhaps it was the will of His Father that it was not yet time for people to know the deep, amazing mystery of His being, nor yet the wonder of His mission on earth. I wonder if—if Jesus pressed the question for deeper understanding. The way Matthew tells the story He did, and Peter obviously didn't understand his own answer.

Jesus didn't wait for a question. He moved on, making a statement without a question to precipitate it. He reinforced Peter's confession, "You are the Christ of God," with an explanation of the demands made upon Him by the truth of His Christhood. Here is the answer:

A. "The Son of Man must suffer many things, and be rejected by the elders and chief priests and scribes, and be killed, and on the third day be raised."

That is a terribly hard answer to a difficult question. Suffer? Rejected? Killed? Raised? Those are hardly words by which to understand the nature of the Christ of God! This is a heady riddle, this answer searching for a question. What might the question be?

Q. Who is Christ?

The answer doesn't fit the question, and just now is not relevant.

Q. What is Christ?

Again, the answer must determine the question here. It must be the proper question to the answer.

Q. Why is Christ?

Maybe that's the question. If you bring together the pieces of the great puzzle Christ posed for them, then something of the "why" question and the "suffering and death" answer may make an acceptable union. "The Son of Man came not to be ministered to, but to serve," He said. "The Son of Man has come to seek and to save those who were lost," He said. "The Son of Man must suffer, die and rise again."

Q. Why, Jesus? Why?

The sinful world, sinful humanity, sinners—are without hope. It has been so since time's beginning. The terrible judgment of God has been spoken. Under it every sinner merits only judgment to perdition, nothing less. Yet, God loved all sinners, for they were His creation. The Father's love and judgment were in irresolvable tension. In order to relieve the tension and satisfy both God's love and God's justice "The Son of Man must suffer many things, and be rejected . . . and be killed, and on the third day be raised." The cross and all its implications satisfied God's justice and became at once God's supreme glory, the mighty manifestation of God's immutable love. That's why. Jesus set His face to Jerusalem. He faced the Gethsemane prayer hours. He was excommunicated by His church. He was executed by Pontius Pilate. He redeemed the world. On the third day He rose again, the Conqueror. He ascended into heaven to reign as Lord. He sent the Holy Spirit.

But at Caesarea Philippi Peter was not ready for the whole answer. He undoubtedly tried to fathom the answer. His mind sought for the question it posited. Only when he was filled with the outpoured Spirit did the answer and the question come together for Peter. It was Peter who put together the first sermon for the Christian Church and preached it on Founders Day, the day of Pentevost.

Your Witness

In the courtroom the drama requires that the prosecution turn the witness over to the defense. "Your witness," he says. The defense begins his questions, hoping to break down the testimony of the witness.

We have been baptized. We have been educated in the faith. We make public affirmation of it in the words of the Apostles'

Creed. By our presence here in the community this morning, we give evidence (unless you are searching for answers) that we are "an answer" for the world's questions. The time comes at last when the Holy Spirit and the church turn us over to the world. "Your witness, world." In the trial before Caiaphas Jesus did that. "Ask them which heard Me, for in secret have I said nothing." Caiaphas didn't take Jesus up on His offer. The world may not see us as answers waiting for questions, and therefore may not ask questions—out loud. The world is always wondering none the less, for it cannot understand what makes us different from the way it is. "Why are you always happy?" "What makes you tick?" "Don't you ever get angry?" "How can you forgive that?" And even a question like, "How can you be such a hypocrite?" or, "How can you say one thing and do another?"

We are bid to be ready to make answer about our Lord to anyone who asks. But if "the world" does not ask the question, our Lord has another plan. On the mountain top, from which He ascended into glory, He commissioned His people to "Go into all the world and witness the Gospel to every creature." Don't wait for the world to ask. Tell the world, for you are the carrier of the Good News of the world's salvation to the world. It is Christ who says to the world: "Your witness." Are you ready for cross-examination?

Amen.

SUNDAY OF THE PASSION (PALM SUNDAY)

Cross Winds

Luke 19:29-40 (RSV)

Dear Friends,

They didn't let the donkey's feet touch the ground. "It's the King," they cried. "He's our King." They hacked palm branches from the nearest trees; they unwound their sashes; they fairly covered the narrow street into the city to keep the donkey's feet from the dusty cobblestones. They were in a jovial mood. You could hear the lilt in their voices as they called out to Him, "Blessed be the King who comes in the name of the Lord!" and "Peace in heaven and glory in the highest!" What an exciting day for them—and for Jesus!

Praise God, the holy Christian church, including thousands upon thousands of little Christian communities, is still singing the praises of King Jesus. We have decked our chancel with palms. We have picked out the most exciting hymns we could. We want to add our voices to the lusty voices of the first triumphal entry. Jesus is Lord! Jesus is King! "Hosanna in the highest! Blessed is He that cometh in the name of the Lord."

Crosswinds were blowing in that first Palm Sunday parade. Would that it was all as jubilant as it appeared on the surface. For a little while this morning, let me take the wind out of the billowing sails of the Palm Sunday story. There are contrary breezes blowing. The crosswinds set the heart of Jesus on edge.

Contrary Wind
THE END OF THE JERUSALEM ROAD

Even as Jesus accepted the cheering of the multitudes, He was conscious of the high purpose that brought Him to the capital city. The time had come for the final phase of the divine plan for redemption to be set in motion. Let the people shout "Hosanna!" to their heart's content. At the end of the road that

Jesus traveled He could see the cross and death. Let them shout "Blessed is the King who comes in the name of the Lord" just now. Before the week is out Caiaphas will accuse Him before Pilate of Kingship and press for the death penalty because of it. Let the people cry "Peace in heaven and glory in the highest" (shades of the angel chorus at His birth!), the donkey's feet would move Him closer and ever closer to the damnation He came to take in His own body on the tree.

One thing is certain, the structures had been set for His arrest. The raising of Lazarus had proven one miracle too many for the chief priests and their crowd. When Lazarus came out of the tomb, their patience with Jesus snapped. They became obsessed with the single idea to remove Him from the scene. Jesus' triumphant procession actually bordered on the defiant. Jesus was making Himself available to His enemies. He was very much aware of what He was doing. Step by step, cheer by cheer, He moved into the city and to His death.

Contrary Wind
JESUS OR CHRIST?

Sorting out the clues strewn through the Gospels and again in St. Paul, by the Holy Spirit, brought the early church to the mystery of the uniqueness of Christ. The Apostles' Creed says it well in the familiar words, "He was conceived by the Holy Ghost, born of the Virgin Mary." From earliest times in the Christian Church Jesus is said to have "two natures," divine and human. He is called by Christians the "God-Man." He came from God; He returned to God. Scriptures ascribe to Him divine names, divine characteristics, divine prerogatives. They give to Him divine honor and glory. At the same time they will not let us forget that He is a human being. They describe Him as one having all the natural human functions. He ate; He wept; He loved. They point out that "His soul was exceeding sorrowful, even unto death." The Gospels carefully build up the evidence for His deity. He spoke as one having authority; He controlled the roaring seas; He called the dead to life. As carefully they seek to establish His humanity. A manger served as His crib. He had nowhere to lay His head. He hungered; He thirsted; He suffered; He died.

Do not forget His two natures on Palm Sunday. Luke alerts us to them. The text: "[they] began to rejoice and praise God with a loud voice for all the mighty works that they had seen." For all the mighty works that they had seen! For His works they praise God. At Caesarea Philippi the disciples answered Jesus' question about the success of His communication, "Some say You are John the Baptist, or Moses, or Elijah." The crowds were willing to go a long way, but not far enough. In spite of the signs, in spite of the authority, they were able to think of Him as the great Old Testament lawgiver, or a prophet returned from long ago. Not the Messiah! Not the Christ! On the streets of Jerusalem, on the first Palm Sunday, they understood Jesus no better. They praised God for the mighty works that they had seen.

The best they could do, those parade watchers in the holy city, was to see *Jesus* the Man from up near Nazareth, who healed their sick, filled their stomachs, and made them feel good with His endless story telling. They praised *Jesus;* they honored *Jesus;* they were thrilled that *Jesus* had come into their city and their lives. "Blessed is the King who comes in the name of the Lord." Let *Jesus* be our Champion; let us make *Jesus* our King. All their shouting, all their rejoicing, all their fine words—mean only that Jesus had not reached them. They hadn't grasped the *Christ;* they couldn't see deeply enough into Him to see the Messiah. The discourses, the miracles, the tender loving care He had given them had only human origins after all. So they praise *Jesus* and ignore the *Christ!,* all, says St. Luke, because of the mighty works which they had seen.

It is not really so difficult to understand that these same people could cry "Crucify Him" later in the week. On Palm Sunday they had given Him mighty allegiance because of His mighty works. When they saw Him bound and bleeding, lifting no hand, speaking no King-kind of words to save Himself, they were certain they had been fooled. And no one takes being made a fool lightly. Ah, the crosswinds blow contrary. They whip around and demand the sails be trimmed. Jesus Christ holds steady to the course only by strictest discipline, only by perfect obedience.

Jesus sat erect upon the colt. When the Pharisees in the

crowd, who knew no more or saw no more than the multitude of people, called out, "Master, rebuke Your disciples," Jesus replied, "If these were silent, the very stones would cry out." If God's hour had arrived and the time of the great offering was at hand, then Jesus must make Himself available to the ecclesiastical authorities. "Let the people rejoice and shout their praise for they raise Me to visibility and make possible the sacrifice of the Lamb for the sins of the world. If they do not, by their boisterous praises make My presence known, then the stones will, for the plan has been set in motion."

Ride on, ride on in majesty,
In lowly pomp ride on to die!

Cross Winds
PALM SUNDAY PALMS

We are privileged to live on this side of Calvary and the open tomb. It is easy for us to second-guess the Jerusalemites, St. Luke, or even the Holy Spirit in matters that are written concerning those people so long ago. It is more essential for us to examine ourselves and our faith in the midst of our boisterous Palm Sunday singing. There are test questions for 20th-century Christians, no different from those asked by the church through the years of its history. Do you believe that you are a sinner? Do you believe that you are damned unless you repent and believe? Do you believe in God, the Father, Creator, Preserver, and Judge? Do you believe in Jesus Christ, Son of the living God, Redeemer and Lord? Do you believe in the Holy Ghost, Sanctifier? Do you understand the implications of discipleship? of the mission of the church, as servant and as witness to the world? These are questions vital to your soul and vital to the Kingdom of God! If you have Jesus without Christ you have set yourself a collision course. If you have notions that faithfulness of Jesus will bring you a "bed of ease," disabuse yourself of such a notion. If you have understanding and faith in the Christ, then you are ready to "suffer together with Him, to die and be buried with Him, to rise and live with Him." Then you can join the hosts who offer Him praise here below. Only, unlike the people of Jerusalem, please sing the Christmas song correctly, "Glory to God in the highest, and *on earth* peace, good will to men."

It is Palm Sunday. In just a little while we will say our Sunday prayers. Following the prayers we will stand, and, with feet planted firmly, confess our faith in the words of the Apostles' Creed. This is our "stand-up-and-be-counted" moment. This is our affirmation of God in us, of our motivating force. This is the faith for which tens of thousands have moved into martyrdom and by which thousands of thousands have moved into glory. "I believe!" This is the faith for which I will forfeit my life. When the Creed is finished, will you come, beginning from the rear benches, to the altar. Here receive a portion of palm, fall into the procession behind the crucifer and proceed out of the church, into the "world" where you will be living out your faith this week. Outside please gather about the Processional cross, and when all of you are gathered, I will ask the Lord's blessing to be upon you, for it is from here that you proceed to do your Christian life in the place where God has willed you should.

On the first Palm Sunday the multitude followed Jesus to Pilate's judgment seat to cry for the death penalty. Now the procession is from the cross to serve the living God, to the death if necessary, as we journey to the crown. Let our procession be no less joyous than was the first one; let it be joyous and in praise of God for all the right reasons. And, as the old Gaelic blessing has it, "May the wind be always on your back."

Amen.

MAUNDY THURSDAY

Cross Roads

Luke 22:19-20 (RSV)

Dear Friends,

Maundy Thursday services are family affairs. It has been like that in Christian circles since Jesus, so long ago, sat down with His disciples, and in the intimacy of their little community, ate the Passover with them. The Gospel accounts of the Upper Room experience have a unique warmth about them. Even with Judas at the table, the discussion about who should be greatest among them and the little argument over the foot washing, the overriding mood of the Upper Room is quiet love. This is so, undoubtedly because Jesus loved, and apart from the cross itself, never was His love so profoundly expressed. Listen to the discourses, watch the foot washing, pray the High Priestly Prayer, sit at dinner with the twelve—it is the love reaching out from the heart of Jesus that supplies the deliberate, quiet, warm mood at that Passover celebration.

Let there be this night in our service a similar quiet warmth—and for the same reason. Our Friend Jesus has both promised it and is fulfilling His promise to be present with us this night and each time we gather. The love with which He loved His disciples, enhanced now by the accomplished redemption, has not changed. Or if there is change it is our ability on this side of the redemption, to love Him in return. Loving Him enhances our determination to love each other.

I understand right enough who we are. We are people. We are flesh and blood men and women. We have, because of the Old Adam in us, thoughts, words, deeds quite unbecoming children of God. There are among us people who argue about who should have the greatest honor in glory (one way or another), and people who wouldn't have Jesus wash their feet, and, God forbid, people ready to sell Him for 30 pieces of silver.

Not one of us measures up to the demands of the Ten Commandments. Who of us has not betrayed God, or soiled His name, or desecrated His Word? Who of us has not rebelled against authority, or dared to hate, or adulterated, or stolen, or gossiped or connived. Measured against the Ten Commandments, not one of us stands free. We are sinners and condemned.

Measured against the Lord's Prayer, if that were our yardstick, we fail. All of us fail. Have we properly hallowed the name of our Lord? Have we consistently worked for the coming of His Kingdom? Are we content with the daily bread for which we pray? Do we forgive every trespass of any brother against us? Have we secured ourselves in temptation and been consistently strong in the face of evil? "Pray as if only God existed, then live as if only you existed," Luther suggested. Too often we compartmentalize, putting God carefully in one box, our life in another. We come off as sinners and are judged again.

The Beatitudes might be used for a check list, considering such words as "humbleminded, sorrowful, claiming nothing, hungry for goodness, merciful, sincere, peacemakers, and forgiving." We soon betray who and what we are. St. Paul's lists of marks for Christians are a frightening check list, too. "Husbands love your wives! Wives submit yourselves to your husbands! It is right for you to pay taxes! Keep out of debt altogether! Love the brotherhood! Shoulder one another's burdens!" We bear the marks poorly. The standards set by our Lord in the Old Testament Decalog, the requirements of Jesus for perfection set before us in His biographies, even the expression of the love of Christ in us, quietly and surely condemn us. We are endlessly at a crossroad. Joshua's "Choose ye this day whom ye will serve" is a never-ending call and a never-ending requirement for Christ's people.

Crossroad

Jesus knew these things about the people who sat to eat the Passover with Him on that first Maundy Thursday evening. As they sat at the traditional and sacred meal, He must have looked at each of them. James and John (John even now leaning on His breast) were called the Sons of Thunder because they bellowed so much. He looked at Simon Peter a long time, with patience born of a deep love. His gaze stopped at Thomas, who just wouldn't let himself be taken in. He looked at Judas, who already had negotiated the betrayal and dared to sit at meat with Him. Not one of them was "recommendable"; not one of them merited His or the Father's love. They were all sinners, to a man. They all stood in judgment to a man. Jesus loved them.

It is right there among the Twelve that it happened. Among that unlikely group of men the Old Testament came to an end. He reached for the bread and blessed it. He reached for the cup and consecrated it. "This bread is broken for many," He said. "This cup is the New Covenant in My blood," He said. "This do in remembrance of Me." Right there, amid these twelve sinful men, our Lord held out to them the New Covenant, the New Testament in His body and blood. Just here among these sinners who were to be His apostles, He set a new memorial to Himself. It is an incredible moment. The Old gave way to the New. The bread and wine consecrated for the celebration of the Passover, is consecrated again for the New Testament. The Passover lamb which caused men to look forward to Him, is replaced. He Himself becomes the Lamb. Tonight He will be chosen for sacrifice on the altar of the cross, as He is abandoned by man and God to the awesome terrors of hell. He came to the Cross Road in the Upper Room. Doubting Thomas, betraying Judas, loudmouth John, self-important Peter, sophisticated Nathaniel—they were all there when He changed the direction and the course of the faith.

"Do this for a memorial to Me," He said. The Bible constantly emphasizes the creation of memorials in remembrance of the name of the Lord. The tabernacle with its lavers and its altars, its courts and its holy of holies, and its ceaseless worship has just this purpose: it was the place where God met His people. The temple high on Zion with its gold adornment, its columned courts, its altars of incense, its great curtain separating the holy place, and with the cloud hovering over it, was held most holy for God placed His name there to be remembered. "This do in remembrance of Me," our Lord said as He consecrated the bread and the wine for the holy Sacrament. He caused "His name to be remembered" in the Sacrament. And on this holy night we remember Him, Lord and Savior of us all.

Jesus broke the bread and passed it. Each of them ate of the loaf, understanding by their action that they were one, even as the pieces of bread made one loaf. He passed the chalice of wine and each of them partook of it, a demonstration of their communion with Him whose name the memorial meal bore, and with each other. In the bread and wine, in the body and the blood they were, as Jesus had prayed they might be, one with Him and one with each other.

Cross Road Exit!

They sang a hymn or two then, after the manner of the Jews at Passover. I believe they passed the peace, Jesus going to each one and for a moment holding him close. He moved down the steps from the Upper Room, through the narrow streets, to Gethsemane and its agony, toward the cross and its terror. The New Covenant had been established and the sign and seal had been placed upon it. Now its terms must be met. He would effect the redemption of the souls of all humanity, somewhere out beyond the love and protection of the Father. Exit Judas, with whom the covenant had been sealed by betraying Him. Exit Peter, who had eaten the bread and drunk the wine by denying Him. All of them who had been in the Upper Room so short a time ago, forsook Him and fled. Exit the disciples.

I wonder how we will fare after our little hour with Jesus and with each other. Already we have made confession and heard the absolution. The sacred words of Scripture have been read. We have sung our hymns. In just a few minutes we will come to the Lord's table, where He has "caused His name to be remembered there," and have renewed for us and with us, the Covenant with our Lord. This profound moment the whole of what God is in Christ touches each one of us. The whole Passion, the whole heart of our Lord, is concentrated in the bread and wine for each one of us. And we who fail the commandments, who fail the Lord's Prayer and the Beatitudes, we know God loves and forgives us, comforts and encourages us there in the covenant.

Cross Road Enter!

How good it is to know our Lord. We have been at the Sacrament before. Since last we were here, we came to our personal crossroads. For a moment we forgot who we were and where we were going. We turned off the way and spent time being lost for a while. How well we understand Peter who wept bitterly in his lostness or Judas and his, or the men who fled the Garden and theirs. But how good it is to know our Lord. For the road He has bid us travel is filled with "Enter" signs. "Come unto Me all ye that labor and are heavy laden," He said. "Who shall lay anything to God's elect. It is God that justifies!" "And while he was yet a long way off, his father ran and kissed him." "Come for all things are now ready." We who are so often lost are urged each time to return to be touched by our Lord in His Word, in the blessed Sacrament, that we might know God's love all over again.

We are a family, gathered here this very special evening. Not one of us is without sin, not one. We are forgiven by the grace of God in Christ, every one of us. We are gathered as a most unlikely family, but family none the less in the Christ and Lord whom we share. In Him, with Him, for Him, we break this bread together here in time, that we may all break it new with Him in His Father's house in glory.

Amen.

GOOD FRIDAY

Cross Currents

John 3:16 (RSV)

Dear Friends,

For the swimmer caught in the unpredictable ocean current, the best advice is to move with the current until it plays itself out, then swim back to shore. Once in the current it is almost impossible to swim against it. Our Lord was caught up in a current that would sweep Him to the cross, carry Him into the judgment of God, and consign Him to the terrors of hell. There was no way in which He could extricate Himself from the relentless forces that swept Him along—no way, that is, if He were to remain the obedient Son and Servant of the Father.

There are lesser currents in the Passion Story, crossing and amplifying the main current. Such a current is suggested by the handwashing episode in the trial of our Lord before Pontius Pilate. When all the fair and foul means Pilate could think of to release Jesus had been explored, he called for water and washed his hands before the crowd. During his years in Palestine, Pilate had done his homework in his effort to rule these people with understanding. In the fifth book of Moses, he remembered, a law had been set down concerning the discovery of an obviously murdered body lying somewhere between two villages. If the murderer could not be identified, the village to which the body was closest must take blame for the murder, while the other villagers washed their hands and said, "Our hands did not shed this blood" (Deut. 21:1-9). Thus Pilate washed his hands before them all—and they answered, "His blood be on us and on our children!" (Matt. 27:25) This little crosscurrent in the Passion story raises the question, "Who killed Jesus?" "Who must take the blame for the 'murder'?" No one wants the blame; the responsibility must be laid at someone's tent door.

Cross Current, Caiaphas (The Church)

It is easiest to blame Caiaphas and the Pharisees and scribes who engineered and "railroaded" Jesus out to the cross. There is no question of their involvement; for they took counsel how they might put Him to death. Caiaphas made a speech at one of their clandestine meetings. "It is expedient for one Man to die for all," he said. No one asked why "One should die for all." Caiaphas laid out the procedures. Jesus was arrested on schedule. The search for at least two witnesses to agree gave him a good case of agenda anxiety. He knew the Passover was very close and the elimination of "the one Man" had to be accomplished before the sundown marking the beginning of the holy observance. They found cause that seemed to give them the privilege of labeling Jesus a blasphemer and therefore, by a vote of those present, "guilty of death."

They took their Prisoner to Pontius Pilate, since they were not permitted to administer the death penalty. There they accused Jesus vehemently of many crimes against the state. So insistent were their voices that Pilate, fearful that he might lose the last little bit of rapport he had with them, gave in to them. He washed his hands of the whole matter—and allowed (ordered) the crucifixion.

Caiaphas was on the Golgotha scene. He relieved his guilt feelings, for the moment at least, by joining in the mockery hurled at the crucified Christ. He was back with Pilate just before sundown announced the Passover, demanding that the tomb where they had laid the body of Jesus for its final rest be sealed over Pilate's insignia, "lest they come and steal the body." The "body" seems terribly close to Caiaphas. But we cannot wash our hands yet, for there are other "villages," other people in the Passion drama, whose closeness must be measured.

It is by no means a footnote to add the dimension that Caiaphas and company were/are the church. He represents the Covenant people, whom God so long ago had led out of Egypt, whom God had loved through the centuries in spite of themselves. It is easy to make a case, because of Caiaphas, for the involvement of the church in the murder of the Christ. But wait, we have other measurements to make.

Cross Current, Herod (the Nation')

Herod, tetrarch of Galilee, had opportunity to declare Jesus innocent and set Him free. When Jesus stood before him his oriental mind thought He might be John the Baptist back from the dead to haunt him. He demanded miracles; Jesus was silent. When Herod moved past his fears of Christ, he used Christ for a political power play. He dressed Him in a toga, symbol and sign of a political aspirant, and sent Him back to Pilate. Pilate laughed and made a mental note to have Herod in for dinner soon. Herod certainly must come into question in the search for the people or person responsible for the death of Jesus. But do not wash your hands yet!

Herod, it must be said, represented his nation. God had made a nation out of His Covenant people. He gave them the land, flowing, it is said, with milk and honey. He nourished the little nation through the centuries. It had endured for 1,500 years because of His sheer blessing. The case against the nation in the death of Jesus is easily made. Do not, however, call for basin and towel, for we must measure the distance the body on the cross is from Pontius Pilate.

Cross Current, Pilate (Humanity)

Every time we profess our faith in the words of the Creed, we lay the responsibility for the suffering and death of Jesus at the feet of Pontius Pilate. He examined Jesus in the best legal tradition. He found Him innocent. He played on the sympathy of the people with the "Behold the Man" ploy. He reached for Jesus' freedom with the prisoner-release tradition. But the insistent voices of the priests, the persistent "Crucify Him" of the people, finally broke him down. He called for water, and washed his hands. "Go ahead," he said, "you take the responsibility." Pilate let an innocent Man die. The case against Pilate is terribly strong.

As Pilate in his office represented all of the Roman world, so in Scripture he represents humanity. In Pilate all of humanity surges against Jesus and in an enormous indifference to Him expunges Him from its midst. But wait, this is still not the time for washing.

Cross Current, You and Me

It may well be that the men who people the Passion story of Jesus are caught up in the plan for the salvation of the world, in order to facilitate the plan for our salvation by the death of Jesus. It is an axiom of the holy faith that Jesus died for my sins. "Christ has utterly wiped out the damning evidence of broken laws and commandments which always hung over our heads, and has completely annulled it by nailing it over His own head on the cross." (Colossians 2:14, Phillips) The poet says it in one of our hymns:

> Who is it that hath bruised Thee?
> Who hath so sore abused Thee
>   And caused Thee all Thy woe?
> While we must make confession
> Of sin and dire transgression,
>   Thou deeds of evil dost not know.
>
> *TLH* 171, 3

God's immutable law hangs over our heads. It condemns us at every turn, for there is not a commandment in it, not a demand of it that we have not broken. Christ died for my sins. He died for your sins. He died for the sins of Caiaphas, Judas, Pilate, the man with palsy, and the lepers on the dusty road outside Jerusalem.

But wait, do not dip your fingers into the water, not yet.

Cross Current, the Father

The core of the Gospel is that God the Father sent Jesus to the cross. "Go forth, My Son," we sing in one of our great Lenten hymns, and with good reason. Jesus said it over and over, "As My Father has sent Me." God the Father sent Jesus Christ, His only Son our Lord, to the cross. He set the demands for the redemption of humanity. Those demands required fulfilling the law. They required suffering. They required accepting judgment including the terror and torment of hell.

St. Matthew puts the stark drama of Calvary into two sentences. "Now from the sixth hour there was darkness over all the land until the ninth hour. And about the ninth hour Jesus cried with a loud voice, 'Eli, Eli, lama sabachthani?' that is, 'My

God, My God, why hast Thou forsaken Me?' " (RSV). Here is the picture. About high noon the Father gave order to the angels to cover the scene on Calvary with a dark cloud (I speak in very human terms). So awesome was the sight on Calvary that the Father could not, would not, dared not, watch it. The Father was abandoning His Son. Nor dare the Son know the Father near. He had by the nature of sin and the judgment against it moved out of the Father's love sphere and into hell. He took upon Himself the damnation of the whole world. He suffered every person's sins. Nails and flies and mockery we can understand; but we can only guess at the awesome terror of the ultimate penalty. Christ was in hell on Calvary. The Father who met Him in prayers on the mountain tops did not come near Him on this mountain top. The Father abandoned His Son to hell. In hell, the Son lifted up His eyes and saw—only the dark cloud. The minutes dragged on, each one an eternity for the Father on the judgment seat, each one an eternity for the Son in hell. Then, at three o'clock, Christ cried His agonizing cry, certainly the most terrifying words that have ever been spoken. "My God, My God, why hast Thou forsaken Me?" A few moments later He cried with a loud voice and died.

All these terrifying thoughts about God grow out of our text for this Good Friday. The darkness, the cry, the silence of God the Father over against His Son all lump together into that deeply profound word, "love." God so "loved" the world! In love for us the Father set up the currents that would carry His Son to the cross, no, much farther than that—to hell. In love for the world, for us, He caused the darkness, lest He see the agony of His Son, lest His Son know His agony. God's love made enormous demands—on God. Because of His love our sins are forgiven. Because of His love we will not perish, but have everlasting life. Because of His so great love we have in us the hope of glory.

Wash your hands now. The body of Christ lies closest to the Father's tent.

Amen.

EASTER

Alleluia! Alleluia! Alleluia!
The strife is o'er, the battle done;
Now is the Victor's triumph won;
Now be the song of praise begun.
Alleluia!*

The Cross—the Crown

Introduction to the text: The opening chapter of St. John's Revelation contains the vision into which John was caught on a Lord's Day somewhere near the end of his life on the Isle of Patmos. The vision began with Christ standing front and center among the sevenfold candlesticks. Christ announced Himself to John as the "Alpha and Omega," the Author of the vision. John reports how, beholding the reigning and ruling Christ for the first time, "he fell at His feet as though dead." Christ identified Himself—and it is this identification-revelation which is the text for us this Easter morning.

Revelation 1:17b-18 (RSV)

Dear Friends,
This text gives occasion to recall the Passion events in the life of Jesus Christ, the First and the Last, who speaks in it. Easter makes sense only in the light of the events that produced it. Many of you, for reasons best known to yourself, could not be present at the Lent and Holy Week services, and therefore are without prolog to this day's celebration, which can best be understood in its context.

The Cross

There is a "theological" context that is basic to Easter. Mankind is collectively and individually sinful. No man could

*See note appended at end.

dare to stand up before the divine tribunal and expect acquittal in his own right. We are all sinners who have violated the will and law of God and can anticipate only death and hell at the end of our lives. God is just. But God "so loved the world," God is so filled with grace and mercy, that He devised the plan by which the sinner might be freed from the judgment against him and have heaven with all its glory as a free gift from God at the end of his life. The plan necessitated the substitution of Another in our stead, both at the judgment and under the judgment. God's only-begotten and beloved Son accepted that role. He would die for us and for all humanity. That is why in our text Christ can say: "I died," for He died under the judgment of God for us.

A second aspect basic to Easter is the historical context in which it occurs. The biographies of Jesus (known as the Gospels), in a most graphic yet restrained way, tell how Jesus approached the impending judgment with prayer at Gethsemane, how He was placed outside the law by the church, the nation, humanity, and finally and horribly by God the Father Himself. "My God, My God!" Christ cried, "why have You forsaken Me!" Then, having accomplished our redemption, He commended Himself to His Father, cried with a loud voice, and "yielded up His breath." That is why in our text the Alpha and Omega can say, "I died."

Easter is the climax to the "theological" context. After three days in the tomb Christ rose again from the dead. On Good Friday night they might have called Him charlatan and fake. They might have said it was all talk and magic. The resurrection, Christ absolutely alive and well, is the vindication of His life, of His message about the Father's love and forgiveness, of His miracles, and of His promises. Easter is the epitome, the crowning, of all Christian theology. That is why Christ can say in our text, "I died, and behold, I am alive for evermore."

The historical context relates the facts surrounding His resurrection. Early on the day following the Sabbath His followers came, found the empty grave and the winding sheets and the angels. Almost as early Christ came to find His followers—Mary in the garden and Peter and the Emmaus disciples. Historically there was no question. "Behold, He is alive forevermore."

In the text, in the vision of St. John, the "First and the Last," that is, the Christ, claims the keys of death and hell. Before the book of Revelation is finished, the reader will understand that death in Christ is gain. The noble army of martyrs walks the pages of Revelation and moves through death with waving palm branches, symbol of martyrdom, but more, symbol of triumph in Christ who opened for every witness the doors of death and shut to them the doors of hell. Somewhere near the end of the Revelation we are assured the gates of hell with Satan inside will be locked forever.

The Scripture lines up our enemies: death and hell and life. They are the great barriers to man's peace in time and eternity. They loom before him like specters. They are unlockable gates of mystery and terror. What lies beyond death? What are the terrors of hell? Is even life tolerable? Then cometh the Victor, the Barrier Breaker. Then cometh Christ our Lord.

In Christ the barriers break and tumble to the ground. "Death," we cry with St. Paul, "where is your sting, where, grave, your victory?" and "Thanks be to God who giveth us the victory through our Lord Jesus Christ." Christ holds the keys of death! The dread of perdition is terribly real for the convinced and convicted sinner. The law screams down at him, condemning and assigning him to hell. The prospect is awesome in its terror. "Being in torment," Jesus said of the rich man in hell in one of His parables. Christ holds the keys to hell. The sinner, who stands with Christ is safe, for the power of hell and Satan were broken at the cross.

The Victory

This now is the picture since Good Friday (retold with faltering words and poetic license). Christ and His holy retinue move toward the very gates of hell. (St. Peter tells us that "He went and preached to the spirits in prison" [1 Peter 3:19].) We have celebrated the pre-Easter event in our Credo, in the phrase, "He descended into hell." The procession is majestic, Satan is vanquished; *Christ* is Victor! Behind the great gates the spirits in prison tremble. Satan himself cowers behind its forbidding walls. The Victor signals the herald angel near the head of the great column of angelic hosts.

> Herald: Lift up your heads, O ye gates, and be ye lift up, ye everlasting doors, and the King of Glory shall come in.

There is silence for a moment, and the sentry of hell's gates cries out, "Who is the King of Glory?" The herald gives answer:

> Herald: The Lord strong and mighty, the Lord mighty in battle! Lift up your heads, O ye gates, and be ye lift up, ye everlasting doors, and the King of Glory shall come in.

Again the sentry on hell's walls cries: "Who is this King of Glory?" And the herald answers once again:

> Herald: The Lord of hosts, He is the King of Glory.

Slowly, reluctantly, the gates of hell open and the procession moves in. The Victor "preached to the spirits in prison," then turned and moved on.

> Congregation (singing):
> The Victor did the foe repel;
> He sounded Satan's final knell;
> He closed the yawning gates of hell.
> Alleluia!

The procession proceeded and arrived at the great stronghold called "Death." Death was the last enemy to be conquered. It was conquered by Christ's death and resurrection. Its terror now is gone. It has become a friend. It has become the gateway to eternity and glory for every person in Christ. Death was brought into the world by the first Adam. It is robbed of its victory by the second Adam to become the doorway to the mansions. There looms the city of death, dark and formidable. With full retinue the risen Lord, the Prince of Peace, moves toward the stronghold, so long the terror and the enemy of mankind. Once again the Victor nodded to the herald.

> Herald: Lift up your heads, O ye gates, and be ye lift up, ye everlasting doors. And the King of Glory shall come in.

From behind the formidable doors came the question.

Sentry: Who is the King of Glory?

Herald: The Lord strong and mighty; the Lord mighty in battle.

Lift up your heads, O ye gates, and be ye lift up, ye everlasting doors, and the King of Glory shall come in.

Sentry: Who is the King of Glory?

Herald: The Lord of hosts, He is the King of Glory.

The great doors of death swung open, to reveal to all the faithful the glories of God's paradise.

Congregation (singing):

Death's mightiest pow'rs have done their worst,
And Jesus hath His foes dispersed;
Let shouts of praise and joy outburst.
Alleluia!

The stately procession moved on toward the third day, which would henceforth be known as Easter. Only a few moments remained before the crowing cock should announce the dawn. Only a few moments and Christ would return to the land of the living to walk again among His people. He would show Himself alive to the disciples and to the Marys. He would offer His wounded hands and feet and sides to Thomas. They would know at last the answers to the riddles He had posed. They would have new strength, New purpose, new power. Just now, at dawn, the encounter with the barrier imposed by death and the grave was imminent. The procession paused. The voice of the herald addressing the land of the living could be heard, crystal clear in the morning stillness.

Herald: Lift up your heads, O ye gates, and be ye lift up, ye everlasting doors, and the King of Glory shall come in.

Congregation (the Living): Who is the King of Glory?

Herald: The Lord strong and mighty; the Lord mighty in battle.

Herald: Lift up your heads, O ye gates, and be ye lift up, ye everlasting doors, and the King of Glory shall come in. Who is the King of Glory?

Congregation: The Lord of hosts, He is the King of Glory.

(Singing):
>On the third morn He rose again
>Glorious in majesty to reign;
>Oh, let us swell the joyful strain!
>Alleluia!

The Prince of Life, Christus Emptor, lived among us visibly for forty days after His resurrection. Our brothers saw Him, spoke to Him, were blessed by Him, began to understand Him, loved Him. When the fact of His resurrection was well established, the time came for His return to heaven and His Father. He had slipped into the world in Bethlehem. His task was finished. He had planted the possibility of the new life and the hope of glory in the hearts and minds of His disciples. He commissioned them to spread the good news of His redemption of their lives and their eternal souls. Then, in a most awesome movement, He ascended into the skies and disappeared.

A multitude of angels greeted Him and the great triumphant march of the returning and victorious Son of God moved toward the shining gates of glory. A sentry on a battlement of heaven, at the nodding of the Father, cried out:

>Sentry: Lift up your heads, O ye gates, and be ye lift up, ye everlasting doors, and the King of Glory shall come in.

Congregation (singing):
>He opened Paradise once more,
>He leads the way through heav'ns great door
>Where saints shall praise Him evermore.
>Alleluia!

The Crown

Then before the ranks upon ranks of angels, before the seraphim and cherubim, before the mighty archangels, before all the saints in glory, the Father received the crown of glory from a shimmering angel. He placed it on the Victor's head. "Thank You, My Son," He said, "for Your faithfulness." The saints and angels began the descant melody they had practiced for His return. "Worthy is the Lamb," they sang, "Worthy is the Lamb who was slain, to receive power and wealth and wisdom and might and honor and glory and blessing!"

Crowned, now the victorious Christ returns. "Behold, I stand at the door and knock. If any man hear My voice and open the door, I will come in to him." The Victor comes to you and you and you. And the herald's cry sounds in your ears. He calls to you to open wide the gateway to your heart. "Lift up your heads, O ye gates, and be ye lift up, ye everlasting doors, and the King of Glory shall come in."

Congregation (singing):
Lord, by the stripes which wounded Thee,
From death's dread sting Thy servants free
That we may live and sing to Thee.
Alleluia!

"And He laid His right hand upon me, saying unto me, 'Fear not; I am the First and the Last: I am He that liveth, and was dead; and, behold, I am alive for evermore, Amen.' "

Amen.

Note

The medieval church used Psalm 24 as an Easter psalm. This fact suggests this sermon. The herald and Sentry are voices from the chancel. The Congregation joins in at the appropriate places. Of course, the worship order for the day requires that the Congregation have cues printed out. The cues might be given as follows:

The Office Hymn:
Alleluia! Alleluia! Alleluia!
The strife is o'er, the battle done;
Now is the Victor's triumph won;
Now be the song of praise begun.
Alleluia!

At the triumphal entry into hell:
The Victor did the foe repel;
He sounded Satan's final knell;
He closed the yawning gates of hell.
Alleluia!

At the triumphal procession through death:
Death's mightiest pow'rs have done their worst,

89

And Jesus hath His foes dispersed;
Let shouts of praise and joy outburst.
Alleluia!

The triumphant procession into life:
Herald: Lift up your heads, O ye gates, and be ye lift up, ye everlasting
    doors, and the King of Glory shall come in.
Congregation (the Living): Who is the King of Glory?
Herald: The Lord strong and mighty; the Lord mighty in battle.
    Lift up your heads, O ye gates, and be ye lift up, ye everlasting doors,
    and the King of Glory shall come in.
    Who is the King of Glory?
Congregation: The Lord of hosts, He is the King of Glory.
(Singing):
    On the third morn He rose again
    Glorious in majesty to reign;
    Oh, let us swell the joyful strain!
    Alleluia!

The triumphant procession into Glory:
He opened Paradise once more,
He leads the way through heav'ns great door
Where saints shall praise Him evermore.
Alleluia!

Behold I stand at the door and knock:
Lord, by the stripes which wounded Thee,
From death's dread sting Thy servants free
That we may live and sing to Thee.
Alleluia!

An Order of Service
for
THE FEAST OF EASTER

The Prelude

The Theme Anticipated   Psalm 24

Welcome the King of Glory
A Psalm by David

Leader: The earth is the Lord's and the fullness thereof,

Congregation: **The world and they that dwell therein. For He hath founded it upon the seas, and established it upon the floods.**

Voice: Who shall ascend into the hill of the Lord; or who shall stand in His holy place?

Leader: He that hath clean hands and a pure heart, who hath not lifted up his soul unto vanity nor sworn deceitfully.

Congregation: **He shall receive the blessing from the Lord, and righteousness from the God of his salvation.**

Voice: This is the generation of them that seek Him, that seek Thy face, O Jacob.

The Cleansing (Confession and Absolution)

Pastor: In the name of the Father, the Son, and the Holy Spirit. Amen.

Let us kneel and make confession of our sins that we may by God's grace have clean hands and pure hearts before Him.

(The congregation kneels)

We confess . . .

Congregation: **Gracious God, Father of our Lord Jesus Christ, Who has promised to receive us when we come to Thee, we confess that we have sinned against Thee in thought, word, and deed. We have disobeyed Thy Law and we have not loved our neighbors. Forgive us, O God; free us from sin, and grant that we may live and serve Thee in newness of life; through Jesus Christ our Lord. Amen.**

Pastor: Beloved, God has promised us His mercy, and Christ Jesus has died for our sins and in our stead that we may live in newness of life, and in obedience to His will. There is therefore no condemnation for those who are in Christ Jesus. In the name of the Triune God, I therefore forgive you all your sins.

The Theme   Psalm 24 Continued

(The congregation stands)

Voice: Lift up your heads, O ye gates, and be ye lift up, ye everlasting doors, and the King of Glory shall come in.

Leader: Who is this King of Glory?

Voice: The Lord strong and mighty, the Lord mighty in battle.

Congregation: **Lift up your heads, O ye gates, even lift them up, ye everlasting doors, and the King of Glory shall come in.**

Voice: Who is this King of Glory?

Congregation: **The Lord of hosts, He is the King of Glory.**

The Introit *(responsively, enthusiastically)*

Christ is risen: **Alleluia!**

Why seek ye the living among the dead?: **Alleluia!**

Remember how He spake unto you!: **Alleluia!**

The Son of Man must be crucified and the third day rise again: **Alleluia! Alleluia!**

Thou crownedst Him with glory and honor: **Thou madest Him to have dominion over the works of Thy hands.**

Christ is risen: **Christ is risen indeed! Alleluia!**

The Entrance Hymn   "Jesus Christ Is Risen Today, Alleluia!"

The Prophetic Voice *(responsively)* (From Isaiah/Luke)

Comfort ye, comfort ye my people: **Saith your God.**
Speak ye comfortably to Jerusalem, and cry unto her: **That her warfare is accomplished, and that her iniquity is pardoned; for she hath received of the Lord's hand double for all her sins.**
Therefore the Lord Himself shall give you a sign: **Behold, a virgin shall conceive, and bear a Son, and shall call His name Immanuel, God with us.**
He was wounded for our transgressions; He was bruised for our iniquities: **The chastisement of our peace was upon Him; and with His stripes we are healed.**
For unto us a Child is born, unto us a Son is given, and the government shall be upon His shoulder: **And His name shall be called Wonderful Counselor, the Mighty God, the Everlasting Father, the Prince of Peace.**
And the angel said unto them, "Fear not, for, behold, I bring you good tidings of great joy, which shall be to all people: **For unto you is born this day in the city of David a Savior, which is Christ the Lord."**
And suddenly there was with the angel a multitude of the heavenly host praising God, and saying:

The Gloria in Excelsis *(chanted by congregation)*

The Salutation

V. The Lord be with you.
R. And with thy spirit.

The Prayer for the Day *(prayed together)*

Hallelujah!
Eternal Father,
Whose justice has been satisfied
by the death of Jesus Christ
and Whose acceptance of sacrifice
is announced by His resurrection,
we praise You for our forgiveness through Christ
And thank You for the blessed hope we hold
in Him:
Hallelujah!
Through Jesus Christ, Who with You and the Spirit
alone are worthy of our eternal adoration. Amen.

The Epistle for Easter   1 Corinthians 15:19-28

[The Anthem]

The Gospel   Mark 16:1-8

The Confession of Faith   The Apostles' Creed

The Office Hymn

Alleluia! Alleluia! Alleluia!
The strife is o'er, the battle done;
Now is the Victor's triumph won;
Now be the song of praise begun.
Alleluia!

The Easter Message

The Office Hymn Continued

At the triumphal entry into hell:

The Victor did the foe repel;
He sounded Satan's final knell;
He closed the yawning gates of hell.
Alleluia!

At the triumphal procession through death:

Death's mightiest pow'rs have done their worst,
And Jesus hath His foes dispersed;
Let shouts of praise and joy outburst.
Alleluia!

The triumphal procession into life:

Herald: Lift up your heads, O ye gates, and be ye lift up, ye everlasting
doors, and the King of Glory shall come in.

93

Congregation (the Living):
Who is the King of Glory?

Herald: The Lord strong and mighty, the Lord mighty in battle.
Lift up your heads, O ye gates, even lift them up, ye everlasting doors, and the King of Glory shall come in.
Who is the King of Glory?

The Living: **The Lord of hosts, He is the King of Glory.**

On the third morn He rose again
Glorious in majesty to reign;
Oh, let us swell the joyful strain!
Alleluia!

The triumphal procession into glory:

He opened paradise once more;
He leads the way through heav'n's great door
Where saints shall praise Him evermore.
Alleluia!

Behold I stand at the door and knock:

Lord, by the stripes which wounded Thee,
From death's dread sting Thy servants free
That we may live and sing to Thee,
Alleluia!

The Offertory

Create in me a clean heart, O God . . .

The Offering

The Prayers and Lord's Prayer

The Festival Hymn   "Christ the Lord Is Risen Today"

The Paean of Praise *(responsively, standing)*

The unaccountable numbers of nations and people stand before the Lamb crying: **"Salvation to God which sitteth upon the throne and unto the Lamb forever."**

And all the angels stand gathered round the throne worshiping Him and saying: **"Blessing, and glory, and wisdom, and thanksgiving, and honor, and power, and might be unto our God forever and ever."**

And the creatures on the earth sing a glory song to the Lamb: **"Blessing, and honor, and glory, and power be unto Him that sitteth upon the throne and unto the Lamb forever and ever."**

And the nations say: **"Amen and Amen."**

And the saints and angels say: **"Amen and Amen."**

And the people of the Lamb say: **"Amen and Amen."**

This is the feast of victory for our God: **Alleluia! Alleluia!**
[The Anthem]
The Benediction
The Recessional
the Silent Worship